My Life for Yours

Chronicles of a Caregiver's Unconditional Love

Presented by

Valerie Stancill

DEDICATION

This book is dedicated to my late husband, Benjamin Stancill, and all the caregivers who are overlooked as they give their lives for others.

Crystal,
May this book empower, encourage and inspire you to love deeper and wider.
Be caring
Be patient
Be there

Tonya Helly
Sept. 2020

Table of Content

Acknowledgments

I want to thank God for showing me that "I can do all things through Christ who strengthens me" Philippians 4:13 KJV. I realized I was called for such a time as this, and it was all for a purpose.

I want to thank my late husband, Benjamin Stancill, for showing me that "Pitbull tenacity" is real, God's word is true, and it is always for His purpose and glory.

I want to thank my wonderful daughter and son for being my biggest cheerleaders. I don't know what I do without you both!

CAREGIVER'S PRAYER

Father in the name of Jesus, I ask you to bless each caregiver as they give their life for another. I pray they will be encouraged each day and find the strength to continue to give of themselves with no regret or remorse.

Lord in those moments of depression, anger, becoming overwhelmed that you will allow them to experience the peace of God that passes all understanding, and may their hearts be filled with the love of Christ. I pray that they lean not to their own understanding but allow you to direct their paths. We know our paths are for purpose. So, help us to embrace all that you are doing in us for such a time at this.

I ask you, Lord Jesus, to allow them to find their purpose and their why and know that it is all for your glory.

Lord I ask that you guide them on their journeys. Hold them close to you. Strengthen them when they feel they can no longer hold on. Help them realize you are their refuge and fortress, and they safely trust in you always.

I pray they know you have a plan to prosper and not harm them, but to provide hope and an expected future.

Father, I thank and praise you for all caregivers and their loved ones, in Jesus name I pray, Amen

CHAPTER 1

Unconditional Love A reflection of our life...

It was a fairly nice day when we left to get his stress test. We weren't concerned about the test. After all, he was fine. We were just following the advice of his doctors. Instead our minds were preoccupied with the ribs we planned to eat at my sister's annual After Thanksgiving Party. You see, Harold Washington was the rib master. His ribs were the BEST and every year ,we looked forward to smacking and licking our chops. So, we were not focused on the stress test. We walk in, registered, and sat in the waiting area. This is when different scenarios started playing in my mind. Working in healthcare can be a blessing and a curse because sometimes you know too much I would always try to just be a wife, but the medical training would supersede my wife thoughtsand then I'd become Dr. Stancill. No, I am not a medical doctor, but my degrees are in healthcare.

My husband's doctors thought I was a doctor because I intimidate them by asking too many questions, and knew to much. In fact, one doctor told me that I "knew too much to just be a wife." One of his doctors said "you know too much to just be his wife." My husband had some underlying health issues, but to my knowledge, there was nothing that was not being handled. I was very involved in his care, and his healthcare providers knew that I would hold them accountable. I loved giving them a run for their money. After all, this was my "Sweetie" we are dealing with.

He was taken back for the test. I was trying to be calm and relax, but more and more time passed. Fear started to overtake me because I didn't know what was taking so long! I was visibly agitated when I approached the desk (as "Dr. Stancill") to get answers. Well, I was not expecting to hear that my husband had been directly admitted to the hospital for a litany of tests. We were angry! We wanted to go to the party and eat ribs, and this weekend hospital admission was sure to change our plans. 'This admission was futile," I thought. I knew that on holiday weekends, patients are not likely to see any attending physicians or have any testing done. So, for him to be admitted meant that something was terribly wrong. I had to deal with this frustration, while keeping a sotic face because I didn't want to alarm him. This is the day I went from wife to caregiver. I had a choice to make. Either, I was going to allow my medical knowledge and fears consume me, or I was going to call on my Risen Savior. I didn't have much time to decide because I had to keep the "superhero cape" that my husband was accustomed to, flapping in the wind. He would often say, "I love when you make them squirm." They don't know what to do with you. You make them earn their money" Unbeknownst to me, that was the day my life changed.

Depression began for me on the Friday he was admitted to the hospital. My life quickly spiraled out of control. Life as I knew it would be no more for the next

14 years. I was taking care of my husband, working a full-time job with a two-hour daily commute and occasional out-of-state travel requirements, and working as a part-time entrepreneur. I did not take care of myself because his health came first. I became so ill one day, that I was forced to go to the doctor. My Vitamin D level was so low it was untraceable. The doctor told me that I needed to take time of myself. I attempted to explain, through my tears, that I did not have time to focus on me because my husband was ill. She was too critical about my lack of self-care, so I did not go back to her I was tired, overwhelmed and had to deal with his anger of being ill. He took his frustrations out on me. I was offended because I was doing everything I could to make him happy. I know I could not begin to comprehend how he was feeling, but it still hurt. As we progressed through the years, life became chaotic, challenging, and heart breaking. I felt like I fell into an abyss with no means of resurfacing. My life was now all about him. He was on oxygen 24/7, So, eventually, we only went out for "medical reasons" because the ramifications were hazardous. Due to his lack of oxygen he would have episodes of syncope and I would become

petrified. His physician once told me that "one time he may not get up." Each time he had an episode, I would wonder if that would be the day that he did not get up. I remember I had a little conversation with God telling Him what I wanted. I had these conversations frequently. I said ,"God I want this to stop, we are not doing this anymore" Well, when it happened again, I reminded Him of our conversation. I think I did this as a comfort to me more than anything else. He said "Daughter I got this and you too, but if it makes you feel better to be mad and upset."

Many illnesses, situations and circumstances came from the nucleus of Pulmonary Arterial Hypertension. Things too a turn for the worst when he was placed on dialysis. He hated it so much and I hated how he was treated as a dialysis patient. Patients were just a number. They would sit for four hours and then get up so the next patient could warm the seat. His care was mismanaged, and of course I was not going to tolerate this. I learned how to do his dialysis at home. I am not referring to peritoneal dialysis, but accessing his arterial artery and vein every other day with a 14 g needle. I had everything the dialysis center had, except I cared about his outcome. Oh my God, I loved that man.

During the time I was doing his dialysis I fractured my elbow. He did not want to go back to in center dialysis, so I took care of him with one arm. Believe me, being a caregiver was difficult, and overwhelming. I would do it again if I could have him back. My life no longer was important. I just wanted my husband to be healthy again. My heart ached for him. I wanted to take his place so many times, just so he could remember what it was like to be healthy. As I write this, I am overcome with sadness just from memories of his life. He never complained and fought every day. I don't believe I could have gone through what he did. I find joy in how our love superseded all the cards that were handed to us.

Giving my life for his perpetuated depression, frustration, heartache, suicidal thoughts, becoming overwhelmed and losing my self-identify. Would I do it again, ABSOLUTELY! Giving my life for his was a painful journey, but one that yielded purpose. I will "PHight" in his absence against Pulmonary Arterial Hypertension until I no longer have breath in my body. I promised him... Our scripture, now mine - **Jeremiah**

29:11

For I know the plans I have for you, declares the Lord,
plans to prosper you and not to harm
you, plans to give you hope and a future...

See you at the top my forever love.

CHAPTER 2

Why Me God?

The day that I received the phone call from my biological mother, that she needed me to come to Buffalo and meet with her doctors concerning her health, was one of the worse days of my life. My biological mother gave me up when I was 8 months old and she never looked back. Even though I met her years later, I never thought I would have to travel back and forth from Erie to Buffalo every weekend to see about her. This wasn't something I wanted to do and to be very honest, I wish I never did, because of all the issues that surfaced, since her passing.

When one takes on the responsibility of caring for anyone, there are many challenges. If you already have a family, you must take their feelings into consideration, you must make sure their needs are being met. For me, that was hard. I was raising my grandson and I felt guilty leaving him, to take care of my biological mother, knowing that he needed me and that my adoptive mother wasn't well. I found myself mapping out what each person needed, so that I could be there for my biological mother.

I kept running into obstacles that I didn't even realize existed. Leaving or trying to leave on time, to catch the Greyhound after making sure my family was good and had what they needed. Staying in Buffalo and running back and forth to the doctors, then going back to my biological mother's house which was beyond draining. Understanding that I would have to do this all over again the following weekend.

When thinking about being the "caregiver" for my biological mother, I am not sure if I had any fears. It was more anger than anything else. I was angry, because she had the nerve to ask me, the one she gave away. I was angry, because I had to change my life around to be there, because she didn't want to ask my brother or her sister. I was angry, because I had to be the bigger person and put my feelings on the back burner and act as if I was cool with being there. I often wonder, if I am the only one who felt that way. The answer I now have is NO. I have since had people come to me and say they completely understand how I felt and how I still feel.

Giving up your life for someone else's to be their caregiver, isn't easy at all. You will find yourself hurt, angry and there will be obstacles that will come your way. BUT you can't focus on that. You must put your feelings aside and woman up or man up and get the job done. You must do it in love, which for me, was a huge struggle. Once you have done what was needed, then and only then, will you be able to deal with your unresolved feelings.

The day that my biological mother passed, was more like a release. I was able to do what was expected and deal with my unresolved feelings to move on. We all have a purpose in life and at that time, God's purpose for my life, was to be there for my biological mother.

Continue to **RIP Patricia Atchison**

CHAPTER 3

From Mother to Caregiver: Finding My Peace and Purpose

Consider it pure joy, my brothers and sisters, whenever you face trials of many kinds, because you know that the testing of your faith produces perseverance. Let perseverance finish its work so that you may be mature and complete, not lacking anything" (James 1: 2-4, NIV).

My first experiences with caregiving came early in life. Growing up, I often cared for elderly family members for whom my parents, aunts, and uncles served as primary caregivers. I provided respite care for my parents who cared for my great- grandmother who lived with Alzheimer's disease. There was never a dull moment for me when I provided care for granny. I was responsible for granny's hygiene, preparing meals, and keeping her safe. As a result of living with Alzheimer's disease, Granny did not cognitively function as an adult. Therefore, I was responsible for Granny's hygiene, meal preparation, and overall safety. Normal daily tasks such as bathing and dressing proved challenging because Granny resisted verbally and physically. She would forget that she ate and tell others, including the day facility that she attended, that she had not eaten.

During the time I helped my parents with Granny's care, I did not understand the plight of the family member turned caregiver. Who knew, years later, that I would be thrust into that role again-this time as a mother of three young children living with autism. Upon receiving the diagnosis, I instantly plunged into uncharted waters with depths and dangers I could not see.

When someone recognizes that your child has unique needs and mentions it to you, even if you are aware, it can be devastating. One day a friend commented that my youngest was living with autism impacted me like I was hit by an 18-wheeler truck. I experienced trauma over her comment, even though it was true. My husband and I had just finished having a relaxing day together. Our three young children at the time ages two, three, and seven, had spent the day with a close friend and her family. When we picked the children up, my friend said, "Girl, you know she has autism, right?" Those seven words I will never forget. They shook me to my core. I looked at her and said, "Yes I already know. I am waiting for her to turn two years and six months, before I take her through assessment. I want to give her a chance to grow." The ride home after picking the children up, was the longest ride ever both figuratively and literally. When we got to the car and began the drive home, I said to my husband, you know my girlfriend said, "She has Autism." As the words came out of my mouth, a heaviness filled the van. The hurt and confused look on my husband's face, I will never forget. It was as if we were both in shock. What normally would have been a 20-minute ride home, turned into an hour and a half trip.

Did I see signs? Yes, I did. Did I already know in my heart, that my youngest daughter was living with autism? Yes, I did. Although I already knew there was something going on with her, it still hit me like a ton of bricks to hear someone say that my baby girl had autism. My youngest daughter was assessed at exactly two years and six months of age, on August 19, 2014, one day prior to my 36th birthday. To date, that was one of the most stressful days of my life. At the time, my baby girl had limited verbal skills and her attention span was very short. She was so busy at the assessment that the team had a difficult time getting her to sit and complete tasks. The team relied heavily on my observations and information provided, to determine her levels. She qualified for services in the areas of pre-academics, language and personal social skills, and began to receive in-home support through the Infants and Toddlers Program. This program proved very beneficial in her attainment of early learning skills. I believe early intervention is critical. It is important for your child to have experiences with others such as teachers and therapists, to help facilitate growth. Within two months of qualifying for services, a developmental pediatrician assessed her for autism and the final diagnosis was made three appointments and five months later.

My husband and I were prepared for the diagnosis.

However, you can never prepare enough emotionally to hear a doctor tell you that your child is living with autism. When you hear those words, you can feel your heart breaking. When you have children, you have hopes, dreams and aspirations for them, but now it was as if I was mourning the loss of those dreams, hopes and aspirations. All I felt was the pain, no peace, no purpose. I felt an immediate sense of loss and fear of the unknown. At the time that my youngest was diagnosed, I had no idea that within the next 18 months, all three of my children would be diagnosed as living with Autism Spectrum Disorder. As we went through the referral process for assessment with my middle daughter while she was receiving speech services, autism was the furthest thing from my mind. She was advanced beyond her years, talks, and she is very social. We thought she would qualify for social emotional services, in addition to her speech services because she had some behavioral concerns. The psychologist who assessed my daughter was a jewel. I will be forever grateful for her support. Prior to our meeting to discuss the assessment results, the psychologist sent me the report. I was sitting in my car in the parking lot of a popular chain store when I opened the report and began to read. I was in total shock when the assessment revealed that she was diagnosed with high functioning autism or what would have been diagnosed as Asperger's in years past. As I sat in my car in disbelief of what I was reading, I cried. Pain and grief overwhelmed me. Six months earlier, my youngest daughter was diagnosed with autism now my oldest daughter was living with autism too. Why was his happening to my family? I sat in my car thirty minutes before I could gather myself enough to pull out of the parking lot.

As I reflected on the fact that my middle baby was now diagnosed with Autism, I could not help but think that the problems that my son was experiencing, was due to him living with autism as well. Initially, I had to fight for the school team to assess my son. They did not understand why I wanted him evaluated because he had advanced comprehension and academic performance. The school team did not realize that there were A-typical behaviors that he was exhibiting that did not make sense. For instance, he was a very fussy eater, exhibited severe test anxiety, had a hard time accepting responsibility for his actions, became easily fixated on things like wearing a jacket and book bag, demanded a lot of attention from teachers and was oppositional. He would often have meltdowns and even had a designated classroom to go to when he could not manage in his regular class. Thankfully, the teacher agreed that my son did exhibit some odd behaviors that warranted assessment from the school psychologist. As a result, my son was diagnosed with high-functioning autism, and a 504-plan was developed to help support his needs within the general education environment. I experienced such a feeling of relief. Finally, I had received an answer after years of wondering why he exhibited so many quirky behaviors and regulation and social problems at school. After the relief set in, it hit me, all three of my children were diagnosed and is living with autism. I could not believe it!

There are five stages of grief: denial and isolation, anger, bargaining, depression, and acceptance. I dealt with all except one stage, bargaining, but not in the order listed. Denial and isolation were the hardest to endure. I felt so alone, though I knew that I was not the only parent caring for a child or multiple children on the autism spectrum.

At this point, I had worked with parents and children living with Autism for over 10 years, so I know that this is real and affects many. However, I felt like no one could understand my pain and that, I was on an island all alone.

According to the Center for Disease Control (CDC) one in every 54 children born, live with. autism, and I have three children who represent one out of 59! Really?! Working in the field of special education and seeing families with multiple children living with Autism, I always said if I have one child living with Autism, that I would not have another. After having my third child and recognizing that she was living with Autism, there were signs that her older siblings also displayed indicators of autism. I thought to myself, "Okay God, you have a sense of humor." He heard what I said and did not allow me to have an inkling of an idea with the older two, until my last was born. In retrospect, I thank God for His will and His way. I could not imagine life without my three heartbeats. Feelings of anger and self-blame started to seep into my soul. I was angry because my three children were living with autism and I could not help but to wonder if I did something wrong. Was it because I only carried each of them 38 weeks? Were my girls impacted because they were born so close together, less than a calendar year apart? All kinds of irrational thoughts were running through my head. I knew that autism was a brain-based disorder that my children were born with. So, there was no one to blame. However, my husband and I walked around in a fog for a year. We were totally absorbed by our children and their needs. We didn't take any time to nurture our marriage. We had to get to a place where we were able to balance our needs with those of our children.

It was imperative that we move from the place of pain, denial, anger, and hurt, that the diagnosis of autism brought, which is hard to do, when you have not found your peace. I had no peace with this situation. All I felt was the pain. I now realize that the pain was part of the process and my journey to peace and purpose. "Now may the Lord of peace Himself grant you His peace at all times and in every way [that peace and spiritual well-being that comes to those who walk with Him, regardless of life's circumstances.

"The Lord be with you all." *2 Thessalonians: 3:16*

CHAPTER 4

Diamond In the Rough

I n this season of my life, it feels like I am in an everlasting blizzard. Yes, everything seems to be tremendously cold and deeply frigid. This storm has deeply wounded my soul. There are no words. Only the thoughts of expression could depict my overwhelming emotions of emptiness. The pain I endured was invisible covered by a wardrobe of camouflage. Every accessory added to my attire built the armor that clothed my vulnerability. Although my mind runs swiftly, my feet are stuck in a dangerous place of stagnation. As I look up, hoping to see the rays of the sun and feel its warmth beaming brightly on my face, I only got a glimpse of my broken-down brim. It is the hat that covers and hides my eyes, So they can see, but not be seen. You know the hat an old soldier would wear when he is getting dressed up. It leaves my ears exposed to listen to the noise of the world, depending on the positioning of where it sits. The hat serves as protection for my head, but it is really the stance I took to be the caregiver of a caregiver.

My mother took care of so many as a wife, in standing mother, daughter, sister, aunt, cousin and nurse. She gave of herself unselfishly, no matter the season. I observed this love as she cared for others, but I realized that my mom was losing her shine. So, I made a choice to stand with her, sometimes by her side, other days behind her, and every now and then, I would take the lead. Being a caregiver was not an option, but a choice that came naturally. I did not say yes, but I never expressed the response of no. When you love someone unconditionally, you will do just about anything to get them thru a difficult season. Whether you lose some sleep, have to call out from work or sacrifice your personal time. It was a time of providing my strength to a level of exhaustion, running on fumes becomes the norm. It was a journey of transition, smiles, laughs, sometimes joy, overwhelming emotions, tears, hopelessness, heartbreak, bitterness, anger, and death.

My storm of becoming the caregiver of a caregiver began over 20 years ago. Both of my grandparents struggled with an illness and needed daily assistance. In November 1993, my grandfather passed away. Nine months later, in September 1994, my grandmother transitioned as well. This left my mother to deal with the loss of both of her parents in a short span of time. It was a depressing time, filled with sorrow, and it was not even close to being over. Seeing my mother's tears was heartbreaking. I couldn't ease the pain, so I had to make sure my mom got through this stressful time. However, despite already being in a grieving state, death came knocking again, this time taking my mother's grandmother (my great-grandmother). It was a difficult time. Now, I was carrying the baton, and one year later, my aunt unexpectedly passed away, leaving my mother to care for three small children, whose father was consumed with the use of narcotics. This blizzard was getting increasingly frigid and zero degrees blew in, when my father started having major health issues. It seemed like this storm was never going to end.

Finally, the flowers began to bloom, and you could hear the baby birds chirping high in the trees. Thank the Lord, we could dust ourselves off, but we were wounded. Life was good and for these few years we could breathe and enjoy a place of some normalcy. I continued to stand my baton battered and bent, while slowly moving forward to recover some footage. Just when living life, not just surviving, really began to happen, a bomb dropped down upon my family. My nephew, who was an all-county, all-state football player, was convicted of murder. This situation crushed my parents beyond anything I ever seen them experience. They had raised my nephew from months old. He went from being a joy to be around and the pot of gold at the end of the rainbow on many days, to being caged in a world based on warehousing instead of reform. The charges take a toll on my father physically. However, as my father struggled with his own health, he watched six of his siblings decline mentally, emotionally and physically until their deaths. The storm was back more furious and brutal than ever.

In 2012, caring for a caregiver, became my main objective. Although I did not realize caregiving is what I was doing, it swallowed me whole. My dad was declining in his health due to diabetes. Three days a week, he had to go to dialysis, which was not a comfortable place at all. During these years with all the trials and tribulations, my parents loved and took care of one another the best way they could. When there was a need, I picked up the slack without hesitation. Never did it seem like a burden, I was only doing what they did for me first, giving unconditional love. Looking back, I believe it was a combination of fear and obsession that made me feel as if I always had to be there. My little cousins were without their mother, and I still had both of my parents. Just the thought of losing them scared me to my inner core. I focused on keeping them up and running. If I could keep my Mom motivated and in the game where she felt alive and positive, I was doing great. So, I cared for her, and made sure my dad focused on living beyond his sickness. We were a perfect team! We took care of each other regardless of the difficult days. Some days were harder than others and the struggle is still real to this very day.

While giving of myself to emptiness, I hit a brick wall. When my grandparents passed, I was so focused on making sure my mom was okay, that I forgot about myself. I hid my emotions to the point of becoming suicidal. Yes, I planned to take my life because I didn't express my pain. It is because of the grace of God that I am still standing today. My concern was not about me but the people that I loved. That was the beginning of my self-neglect, and it was now staring me in the face. Unfortunately, I did not recognize it, so I continued doing the same thing, falling short in caring for myself while being there for others. There was a tremendous pain in my heart after losing my grandmother. As I helplessly watched my mother grieve, emptiness consumed me. While stuck mentally, I found a great gift in God during this quarter of my life. What a blessing in trying times.

God was always right by my side to listen when I had no one else to confine in. His arms comforted and strengthened me when I could not stand on my own. Truly a relationship of unconditional love that blossomed into a beautiful Rose. I continued to push through, as I never stopped caring. However, it was becoming apparent something was going on with me. There were many days when I would cry or become angry for no reason. My nerves were shot. My patience was short, and I felt that at any moment, I was going to fall apart. Again, I did not recognize the self-neglect because I was focused on caring for my parents. My goal was to assist my mom, so she was able to do what most would not. I will not say it was easy, but my heart's convictions were strong and clearly see my purpose. Unfortunately, my body was not in agreement with the regiment. I was weighed 277 pounds. So tasks that could've been quick, became cumbersome. Fighting fatigue, shortness of breath, and the extreme pain throughout my body was secondary. It was sad for me, because I was unable to recognize myself in family photos and no one thought about helping. It still was not apparent to me, that I had lost myself in giving so much away to others.

One year after Christmas, I went to my parents' home to take down the tree. The tree had dried out so bad that it was difficult to remove the tree stand. The feeling of frustration took over after fifteen minutes. I lost it! I'm embarrassed to admit it, but I tore the tree up! You would have thought the tree attacked me. I was acting like a straight fool. I had the remnants of stencil all over me. When I finished with that tree, you would have thought I was a Christmas tree ornament. My face was flushed, my nose was red from crying, stencil and glitter was dangling from every part of my body. It was a sight to see! Another episode occurred when I was shampooing my rugs and I had to empty the dirty water out of the machine. I had done this a million times before, of course on this day I could not get the water container back on the shampooer. I lost it completely and my poor shampooer was missing all kinds of parts. Little plastic pieces were all over my den.

You are probably thinking that I was crazy and needed some serious help. Well, it was finally obvious to me that I was exhausted. No one needed to say a word. I was the crime scene of self-neglect. I put myself last, while those I love, were placed first. This was a crushing time dealing with the years of not caring for myself. Through tears, I attempted to put my health first and get my life in order. My stride was short but at a constant pace. I was in disbelief over my health and mental status. Anger started to creep up inside of me because I had not put anything into myself, and the results were horrible. While in the process of putting the pieces of my life back together, devastation was on the horizon.

On April 19, 2017, my dad passed away. My heart shattered. I was numb and confused. The pain was so deep and piercing that even now I struggle not to crumble into pieces. Wow! He is really gone. My heart just dropped into my stomach. I was grieving and one of my main reasons to push everyday was gone. The tragedy was here, and it overwhelmed me. As the months went by, I developed deep feelings of hatred and anger. I was still a caregiver and it appeared that everyone else, except my mother, had gone on with their lives. I was completely at a lost because I gave so much, that the reality was overwhelming. Who could I turn to now? My Mom and I were in this battle alone. After the first year of my Dad's death, I understood my anger was because I felt abandoned because no one came around. Where were my family and friends? I realized, I hurt myself by not finding the strength to see me among all I was giving to others. The pain was real and getting deeper because I felt alone, rejected, used and abused. I poured out my all and I ended up with a broken heart. I was empty. In my emptiness, I just wanted to disappear and never return. The wind was knocked out my sail. I had no fight left in me. Although I needed to kick and scream, I couldn't. It was my decision to give my life for those I loved, especially my Dad.

Almost every day I cried and wanted to find someone to punch, because I was exhausted and no one understood my sacrifice. Waiting on my hero was a fairy tale. I needed to rescue myself. First, I stopped being angry and bitter with the world because I chose to sacrifice due to the unconditional love I had for my parents. Secondly, I stopped trying to push the pain of my father's death on others and embraced it. Last but not least, I refuse to continue in self-neglect. It has been a long rough road of loving while caring, but today it is my declaration. I believe it was God who created me to be a caregiver. This choice was made easily, but the road had many twists and turns. On this August sunny day, I can smile and embrace my pain. So much was sacrificed, and I can admit I lost myself in being a caregiver of a caregiver, but I would do it all over again.

As I shake off the debris of this storm, I proudly say to

Sidney and Violet Goffney, your diamond is coming out of the rough.

In loving memory of my DAD!

CHAPTER 5

Hourglass Sadness

My journey to becoming my father's caregiver was not an easy one. I am the second youngest of my father's "five pack." None of us really had a solid relationship with our father. I had a brother who took his life in the 90s, and I still feel that our father's absence contributed to my brother's untimely death. However, out of all the children, my mother ensured that I maintained a close relationship with my father, even though she was struggling as a single mother of four. There were times when growing up came with hard life lessons that my father should have taught me instead, but he wasn't there. In 2010, I was living in Philadelphia raising two daughters of my own. My father had been staying in Washington D.C. with my two older sisters.

While visiting my mother, she informed me that my father reached out to her to let her know that he was diagnosed with MS (Multiple Sclerosis) and was moving back to Philly. It seemed as soon as he moved back, things went downhill fast. While staying with my sisters, he fell and suffered a stroke, which went untreated. Then, he was diagnosed with brain cancer. That was the final straw.

My mother told me that my father was sick and was going to need was my help. I didn't really know how to feel, and my emotions were all over the place. There were times I wondered if I would cry if he died. All the memories of my childhood he missed out on began to surface. When I needed him he wasn't around or couldn't help because it wasn't a good time. I can't forget the times I sat looking out the window, waiting for him to show up and he didn't. Not to mention, the time I wanted to end it all at 13 and he never noticed. Yet I am expected to take care of him? No, it wasn't fair, and I wasn't taking care of him! My mom begged and pleaded with me, saying he didn't have anyone else. I told her I needed to pray about it. I prayed and it wasn't a one-time prayer either. I prayed, prayed and prayed again. Finally, about a month later, I received the answer I needed. God laid it in my spirit and He said, "I chose you because this is for your healing. Your father could only be who he was, and he had his own struggles, but he also knew you would be the one he could rely on." While I was dealing with my own issues, my father was admitted to hospice care.

When I arrived, I couldn't believe what I saw. The strong man, who was always bigger than life to me, was weak, frail, and barely clinging to life. My heart broke in a thousand pieces, and the guilt was super heavy on my chest. While I was selfishly taking my time to decide if I wanted to help, my father needed me. I wanted every minute back. At that moment, nothing else mattered. I stayed by his side day and night. Adjusting to hospice was a difficult task. Trying to grasp the idea that he was going to starve to death was overwhelming. Even though his body was failing, his mind was still there. So, every day he would beg me to take him out of there. I would lie and say, "As soon as you get stronger, I'll get you out of here," knowing that would never happen. I began to read my poetry that he had never heard, although I had been performing for over five years. We read Bible scriptures and listened to and sung gospel music. We also attended church together. Those were some of our best times together.

I called his siblings and my sisters to advise them of his condition. When my sisters arrived, I met so many nieces and nephews for the first time. They all lived out of town and needed to return home. So, I continued to stay at the hospice facility with my father. I continued to pray, but in my heart, I knew I was losing him. I cried and he consoled me like I was five-years-old again. He rubbed my hand with his fragile hand. He didn't want me to cry, but I couldn't help it. I had been at the hospital for three weeks. My sisters volunteered to come and keep our father company, while I spent New Year's Eve with my kids, whom I had not really seen since the whole ordeal began. My sisters were set to arrive from DC around 2pm. I woke up around 9am and heard a strange rattle that I'd never heard and I will never forget. His breathing was shallow. So, I called my Mom and my sisters who were already in route. I knew this was the day I was dreading. While waiting for everyone to arrive. ...I read scripture to comfort him on his journey. My mother arrived first, and I stepped out so she could say her final goodbyes. Less than two minutes later, she stepped out of the room and said, "He's gone." I was praying my sisters made it in time. Ten minutes later, my sisters arrived.

Although I knew it was coming, I was heartbroken. I was grateful for the time I had with him during his final moments, but it wasn't enough time! I felt guilty for the precious weeks I took deciding if I would forgive him for not being the father I wanted him to be, instead of being the daughter he needed. I also felt guilty for the times he came to Philly to visit, and I selfishly didn't make the time to see him. I missed those moments, and now there was no more time. God's will was done and it was over. Although I was relieved that he was no longer in pain, I wanted a little more time with my father, even if it just was one more minute.

Planning the funeral was stressful. My sisters were out of state, so most of the responsibility fell on my shoulders. I didn't have time to grieve because the arrangements were tedious and overwhelming. I was exhausted from obtaining insurance information, selecting the funeral home, talking to cemetery reps and funeral directors, who were trying to capitalize on the fact that this was my first funeral planning experience. I also had to deal with certain family members, who seemed to be more curious about money. So, I intentionally tried to spend every dime on his services. I managed to have his service on his birthday, January 10, 2012. I could hardly stand because I was emotionally overwhelmed. When I stood to speak, my tongue tied and I could not speak at all. All the emotions I was holding, being strong, finally poured out. I know he would have been proud of me. I still miss him every day, and wish he could have been here to witness all of my accomplishments.

Since then, I went on to be a home health care provider, which gave me a great sense of helping people. When I heard of this anthology, I knew I wanted to tell my father's story. However, in the midst of writing, my mother was diagnosed with pancreatic cancer. I am her support person, so the journey begins again for me. Being strong is not something that can be measured. It's doing what must be done when it must be done even when you're tired, stressed out and emotionally drained. No matter what I thank God for the chance to be in a place to be used to be a blessing to someone else.

CHAPTER 6

It Wasn't Hard Until It Was...

I feel I've been my mother's caregiver all my life. As a child she would only play with dolls that had blue eyes and dark curly hair. My mother would often say, someday I want a little girl with blue eyes and dark curly hair. I feel as if this was the only thing I did right. Unfortunately, it was only when I fulfilled her vision of me that she was happy. It was a heavy responsibility to have her happiness dependent solely on me. Mom lived her entire life in a fantasy world. She had little education. She spent her life mimicking the movie stars of the 20's and 30's. She always presented herself as stunning and immaculate. Her biggest concern was always, "What will people think of us. Our lives were a show.

I knew at a very early age that my curly hair and blue eyes would only get me so far. Perfection was the only way to make my mother happy. I lived in constant fear that I would disappoint her or make her unhappy. So I hid so much from her - pain, sickness and fear. The pressure I was under would break most adults, let alone a kid. Maybe drive them to alcohol, drugs or worse. I dabbled, but my fear of her finding out prevented me from continuing down that road, I knew no other way. "For I know the plans I have for you, declares the Lord, plans to prosper you, and not to harm you, plans to give you hope and a future." - Jeremiah 29:11. The more I tried to make her happy, the more she reminded me of imperfections. When she told me that I was "the biggest disappointment of her life," I just figured I had to work harder and sacrifice more to care for her. By my teen years, I couldn't hold on any longer. My grades slipped, I gained weight, and fulfilled her prophecy of disappointment. I think back on how tormented I was going through that time in my life, when I should have been trying to discover and nurture who I was, instead of forcing myself to please her. "I must keep trying," I would tell myself. "Someday, I'll make her proud." By college, I had no self-esteem, no confidence, and barely enough strength to make it through a day. I was a mess. Then my father died, and I gave up my dreams of becoming a Physician's Assistant so I could stay home from college and keep her company. To this day, people ask if I'm an only child. No, my mother had two children. My younger brother keeps his distance and does the bare minimum. I guess we all have our way of coping.

Mom was 57 when my dad died. From then until she was 94, she always had a boyfriend. She outlived five boyfriends over that time. They would take care of her for a while and take care of her need for attention. She would listen to them and take their advice. So, they were more important then me, especially when I became a less than glamorous ultrasound tech and married a man not of her dreams. She was reluctant to help with our twins and didn't spend a lot of time with them. However, she never missed a hair appointment. During her 70s, Mom was taking care of her mom. She kept my grandmother in her own home and visited twice a day. My mother waited until it was legal and claimed the home for herself, sold it along with her own home, and moved into an apartment. She was very well-off. We never saw a dime, even when my grandmother passed. She was clever. She only shared her plans with her boyfriends. She said she didn't trust me. One of her friends was swindled out of her money by her son. I guess she was afraid I'd do the same. If I had known how that curly-haired, blue-eyed little girl was supposed to turn out when she grew up, maybe life would have been a little easier. I guess my mother never got that far in her fantasy. I helped and supported her when I could, but I always felt a tremendous amount of guilt when I made choices that were against her wishes, like when I converted to Catholicism. Still I held back my impatience, hide my resentment and swallowed my pride when she expressed her disappointment in me. Many days, I had to take her to appointments after little or no sleep following a night shift. The silver lining is that because of how my mother treated me, I learned how to treat others better. If something caused me pain, then it could cause pain for someone else, so I tried not to do it. I realized that she was repeating the treatment that she received. Occasionally, I'd ask her if she knew how hurtful she was she didn't mean if. When my mom reached her 90s, she was angrier than ever at me. She was convinced I was against her. Yet I was still there.

I first noticed her memory failing in 2008. Her ophthalmologist recommended some studies. She was in early stages of dementia. Her boyfriend covered for her when she got lost or accused neighbors of stealing or breaking into her apartment. After a couple of years, I had to step in as her boyfriend's physical health declined. He passed away when Mom was 94. The day before he died, I realized how much my selfish my mother was when he complained of chest pains while being transferred to the hospital by ambulance, and my mother said, thinking of herself as usual, "How do you think I feel?" After her boyfriend died, she continued to decline. I visited her each day in her independent living apartment for two years. She was upset about something every day. It reached a point where I begged and cried on my hands and knees for us to get along. She would stare at me as if I was losing my mind. Throughout her 90s, there were several hospitalizations. Some for injuries, bronchitis, imbalanced electrolytes, vascular insufficiency and vision.

Funny how despite everything, it was always hard to hand over her advanced directive and living will. The phone rang a lot, Mom fought with everyone. When I would see the caller ID on the phone I would cringe. She had become paranoid, belligerent and sometimes violent. She gave the hospital staff a run for their money. During an emergency room visit, I remember sitting motionless while she spoke to me in a way no one should ever speak. After this visit, she had to come live with me. She was up five to ten each night. So I didn't rest, and I became numb as I cleaned poop, food and torn books. A couple of times a week a therapist, nurse, or home health aide would visit for an hour. During my precious hour I fled with the dogs and took a walk. It was the only positive I can take away from those visits. The studies tell caregivers how to care for someone with dementia. However, I wonder if the authors of those studies have cared for someone with dementia full time. Thank goodness my husband was so patient, helpful and understanding. He did his best to keep peace. He would play her favorite music and made up thing a for her to do. Slowly the three of us fell into a routine. Mom helped me with the dishes I miss those pleasant moments.

With dementia you never know when the other shoe is going to drop, and drop it did! I remember exactly what I was doing, where I was, when the neurologist called and said that unless you can be with her 24/7, she needs to be in a locked facility. While the doctor was talking to me, the nurses were beeping in to request my assistance in getting my mother under control. After she settled down, the nurses and I sat down and had a snack and talked. As I was leaving the hospital I felt the need to go to the chapel. The elevator was taking along time and I felt it coming-the scream that I had suppressed for years. So I rushed to the stairwell where I slumped down and sobbed my heart out. A nurse came through to use the stairs. "It's ok," she said to me, "Let it out." During this admission to the hospital, there was pressure to get her out. I couldn't bring her home. So, I was calling everywhere and driving all over, looking for a residence for her. When I found a place, I knew, as her power of attorney her savings could only keep her there for about two years. During that time, there were two episodes where I called everyone thinking the end was near. She pulled through only to fall and break her arm. This led to three months of orthopedic visits that I had to take to. Those two years went fast and suddenly I was faced with the issue of finding her another place to live. This was a real struggle, as I had one week to rearrange her banking, find a place and move her. I can remember sitting in a parking lot praying for the strength to interview another facility. This place was not on my list and I realized God led me there. He continued to answer my prayers as the staff, knowing they couldn't take my mom, suggested a place that would accept my mom without official Medicaid approval and she could move in 24 hours! This was extra amazing, as I was scheduled for bilateral knee replacements in two days. Thank you, Jesus, You did it in 5 days! I think Joshua knows something about how You can stop time. "So the sun stood still, and the moon stopped, till the people had revenge upon their enemies." – Joshua 10:13. When most people talk about caregiving, they think of meals, hygiene and medication. Most overlook the mountains of complicated paperwork including medical and legal documents, applications, finances and insurance. Then there are the countless phone calls to be made and filing deadlines to made. Just recently, I had to submit paperwork to prove my mother is still alive. She is currently 101 years and 3 months old. There is also insult to injury, when you have to do it alone.

Last spring, Mom developed bronchitis. It was quite serious and again I thought it could be the end. I asked a couple friends from my church to come and witness her accept Jesus as her Lord and Savior. Despite her dementia, we truly felt Mom knew and understood everything that was said to her. That day made everything okay. I finally gave her a gift she accepted. What a wonderful day. It has been 5 years since my mother has been in memory care facilities. A steady environment has helped. She has become mellow and proudly introduces me as her wonderful daughter. I waited 65 years to hear it. Yet there is little satisfaction, because it's not coming from the person I grew up with. She is not the person who hurt me. I believe dementia freed her of the hang-ups, shame, and tragedies of her life. I'm glad she is finally happy. Many people say they can't believe I still do what I do for her, considering how she treated me. I go twice a week, wash her clothes, check on her and keep up with the

mountains of paperwork. Maybe I thought I would finally do something to please her. Maybe I remembered the 4th commandment, or maybe I knew I couldn't live with myself, if I treated her the way she treated me. Sometimes I procrastinate visiting my mother. It can be difficult knowing that there is always something that gets me stirred up. One evening, I pulled myself together to go. As I drove, I prayed all would be well. I arrived at the nursing home calm, I put mom's clothes in order, changed her socks and blanket, lowered her roommate's TV and had a short pleasant visit. During that visit, I felt a change, not with my mother or the situation, but the change happened within me. I realized everything is going to be okay. I would be okay. It no longer mattered if I made my mother happy or proud Lately visits now are pleasant and fun. We sing and chat and just enjoy each other's company.

As I was leaving, I passed a woman crying in the hall, who was being comforted by another resident. I stopped to help, and the resident was happy to turn the situation over to me. I had known this woman and her family for more than 50 years. She has memory issues but there are some things that dementia patients don't forget. There was a past event in her life and she was feeling guilt, regret and fear over her past words and actions. Since I knew the family and story, I was able to talk with her and reassure her that Jesus had forgiven her long ago and everything was okay. On my drive home, the Holy Spirit suggested I think about my recent visit and why He pushed me not to postpone. I realized I went not because my mother needed me, but God knew that woman needed me. Thank You, Holy Spirit, for reminding me of my purpose. We are caregivers for all. On 30 April 2020 my mother met Jesus.

CHAPTER 7

Ms. M...

"Ms. M, it's time to get your bath, we are going out today." She responded, "I don't want to get in the tub; I can wash myself, thank you!" This was one of many responses to me, from Ms. M, especially when she did not want my assistance with her self-care. I remember feeling frustrated and brainstorming ways to convince her to do what I had asked of her. I knew I could not make her do anything she did not want to do. However, to properly care for her, I thought, "I have to try and convince her, somehow." After all, I had to remember she was an adult and I had to respect her wishes.

One day, I finally said the right thing. I told her we were going shopping. She would also cooperate if I told her we were going to visit her son. When Ms. M did not feel like going out, however, we would watch television and order takeout. I met Ms. M 25 years ago in December 1994. I was dating her son and we were making plans to marry. He told me that she was not happy that we were dating. From the time I met her, I knew she did not really care for me. After I married her son, my relationship with Ms. M was cordial, but it was not a mother-daughter relationship. No matter what she thought of me, I wanted our children to know their grandmother and have a relationship with her. Years into my marriage, I had a dream that I was taking care of Ms. M, but my husband was not with us in the dream. Back then, I had no clue that my marriage would end, and I would really end up taking care of Ms. M. Years later, when I was asked to care for her, the dream was brought back to my remembrance, and it no longer seemed strange.

Ms. M was 82 years old, when I became her caregiver. She was living on her own when she was diagnosed with dementia. Along with her diagnoses, the doctor prescribed Ms. M several medications, which she refused to take. So, I had to find creative ways to administer her medication. I felt like I was caring for one of my children again. Although sometimes she could remember details of her childhood and early adulthood, Ms. M had short-term and long-term memory loss. So, she was unable to care for herself, and needed 24-hour supervision and care. Although, some days she could remember some details of her childhood and very few situations she experienced as a young adult. Sometimes, I think she was more fluid than we originally believed. She would talk about her childhood, and how she experienced trauma from being part of the Japanese concentration camps in California when she was 10-years-old. during the time, at the camps. The theory has not been scientifically proven, but I believed the trauma was part of what was causing the dementia she was experiencing. It is a proven fact, however, that trauma has a major effect on the human brain. We had many conversations about her life; things she enjoyed, places she traveled, and things she learned. Ms. M was a schoolteacher for over 30 years; I admired her. She was the one person in my life, at that time, who encouraged me to pursue teaching. She joked and said the best thing about teaching is June, July and August, summer break. She was funny and never lost her sense of humor.

People say that some things are taught but some things are caught. I believe my time spent with her was not only for her, but for me as well. I needed to learn and "catch" some things from her. I enjoyed talking to her about her experiences as a teacher. I was inspired, so, I pursued teaching for a season. I wanted to honor her, by caring for her. I did not, however, realize what that really meant and how it would change my entire life. I felt my life as I knew it, was on pause and that nothing else mattered but Ms. M and her care. God's Word tells us to be anxious for nothing, (Philippians 4:6), but I could not help but feel a little anxious. I knew very little about dementia and even less about caring for an elderly person with the disease. Every day, I prayed for wisdom and understanding on how to care for her. When I agreed to care for Ms. M, I thought I would have more support than what was received. Initially, caring for Ms. M meant transitioning from a full-time job and working days, nights and weekends, caring for her. I always. looked at her as my mother, so that motivated me to care for her. While in my care, she was my responsibility and I was not only doing it for her son, myself and to honor her, but also to honor God. I felt it was the right thing to do; being an example for my children and her grandchildren meant a lot to me.

I always believed that if my mother became ill, my siblings and I would never place her in a nursing home or another's care. We would take care of her, so that she knew that we loved her and appreciated her. To me, it was just the natural progression of things - we would take care of her in old age, as she took care of us when we were babies and could not care for ourselves. To me, this was honorable. It was my goal to be devoted to her in love and honor her above myself - Romans 12:10 - NIV. There were many days I thought about placing Ms. M in an adult daycare facility for a few hours during the day, so I could take care of errands. Unfortunately, their hours were never convenient for me and the fees were too high. Therefore, Ms. M went everywhere I went. I kept her busy with weekly shopping trips, laundromat visits, church on Sundays, and an occasional breakfast, lunch or dinner out. We also ventured out to several fun events, such as the movies and a paint party. Most of my days were spent on her care and making sure her needs were met in a safe and loving environment. I hoped that plenty of rest, sunlight and proper nutrition would help heal her brain.

At every doctor's appointment, it was confirmed that she was in excellent physical condition. During some visits, the doctor would ask questions about her activity, to establish the progression of the disease. Conveniently, we shared a doctor, but when it came to my care, it was difficult to follow-up. On one occasion, I was not able to find anyone to watch Ms. M for me while I went to the dentist. I took her with me, only to be told that they would not be able to see me. The office staff explained that they could not watch her while I was being seen by the dentist. So, I had to reschedule my appointment. Many of my appointments were rescheduled because very few people could and would watch her. After a while, I felt invisible, like I did not matter. If felt like my life and my well-being was not important. I did not think these, so called, "little things" through, when I was considering becoming Ms. M's caregiver. For instance, there were times when I thought I could run to the store quickly, but suddenly realized that I could not leave Ms. M alone at all.

At times, it was frustrating because it was difficult and

inconvenient to prepare her to go out on a short store run. Our days and store runs had to be carefully planned out in advance. I had to make the most of our time out of the house and make sure I did not overwhelm her, physically. Most days, I was up at 4am because I could hear her stirring in her room. As time progressed, I had to secure the house with an alarm system, to protect her from roaming outside unattended. Taking naps and "sleeping in" was never an option. One day, I left Ms. M with a family member, while I went to church. When I got home, the family member said that she was not a problem at all. When I looked in Ms. M's room, she was not there. I panicked. I had no idea where she had gone. The family member said they thought Ms. M was still in her room. The police came to the house with Ms. M. She had left the house while the family member took a nap. She ended up walking to an area restaurant, ordering coffee, and sitting there for hours. When she did not pay for her coffee and did not leave, the waitress decided to call the police and report it. They realized she was not in her right mind. I was so worried about her. She could not explain to them where she lived. I called the police department to locate her and they brought her home. It was helpful that the situation happened. I learned we could register Ms. M as an elderly dementia patient, with the police department, in the event she roamed from the house again.

As time progressed, waking up early and not getting enough rest and sleep, started to take a toll on my mind and body. By the end of the day, I was exhausted and weary. I used to think, "she's trying to kill me, why is she up so early?" I thought, "If I don't get my proper rest, I will get sick, and who will help me then?" I had to really think about how and when I did things. I reflected on the time when my children were younger and when I stayed home with them. I established routines for their meals, entertainment, education and times of rest. I knew, in order to survive, I had to do the same for Ms. M. If Ms. M had clothing and shoes in her bedroom, she thought she could leave the house and go out on her own. So, I had to remove her belongings and set up her room with things she enjoyed, so she would enjoy spending time there and not leave the house. We watched television shows she enjoyed, I cooked foods I knew she would eat and made sure we had some type of exercise every day.

After establishing a routine and learning Ms. M's ways, I started talking to her about God and how Jesus. loved her. We would talk about how she was feeling and discuss our agenda was for the day. It was like caring for a five-year-old at times, in an adult's body. One day, we took a trip to the laundromat to wash clothes. While we were there, we sat in the car, waiting for our clothes to dry. Someone saw Ms. M sitting in the backseat asking for help through the window. Evidently, they were worried about her being in danger, so they reported the incident to the police. The police pulled up beside me, asked for identification and proceeded to ask a series of questions about Ms. M. They said they needed to confirm a report of suspicious activity. I explained she was my mother-in-law, and I was her caregiver. I thought, *"people need to mind their business."* I was seething with anger because the police were called.

Throughout the years of taking care of Ms. M, if I did not lean on the word of God and pray, I do not believe I would have been able to continue her care. God truly graced me to care for her. One day, a mother at my church volunteered to help me with Ms. M when she could. I would call on her when I went out of town and when I got sick. I appreciated how this family friend loved helping me with Ms. M. She never said no to lending me a hand with her. Our family friend helped refresh me, from time to time. When I was sick, I would sleep for hours, until I had to get Ms. M for the evening. I was so grateful, and I praised God for the extra set of hands. Things were working together for my good, because I love God and I'm called according to His purpose! (Romans 8:28).

My experience as a caregiver, caused me to really understand what unconditional love really is and what it looks like. Caring for Ms. M caused me to grow as a person and helped me realize that we need each other to survive. It made me think about the other relationships in my life and how I really do cherish them. My goal now is to owe no man anything, except to love others: for he who loves another have fulfilled the law, (Romans 13:8). I want to love others like the Bible says to love. Real love is unconditional. God's grace will empower us to love each other like God loved us and gave His son for us. In Creating Sanctuary, by Sandra Bloom, the author cited - We matter deeply to one another for our very well-being... We play such an important role to one another that we cannot do without significant others and remain in health, (p.44) (de Zulueta 1993) (figure 2.1). The Bible declares, though I speak with the tongues of men and angels, but have not love, I have become sounding brass or a clanging cymbal. And though I have the gift of prophecy, and understand all mysteries and all knowledge, and though I have all faith, so that I could remove mountains, but have not love, I am nothing. And though I bestow all my goods to feed the poor, and though I give my body to be burned, but have not love, it profits me nothing, *(1 Corinthians 13:1), NKJV.*

When I was younger, I did not understand this kind of love. My mother was my example, but I did not realize it, until after she was gone. I reflected on the things she taught me, and my siblings and I saw it! I saw love in action from the words she spoke and the things she did for her family and others. As a child I asked, "Mom, why are you doing these things for them?" She always reminded us to love and forgive anyway, no matter what was done to us. She said God would take care of us if we trusted and obeyed Him. We can love like this, no matter what others may do, because the love of God is shed abroad in our hearts by the Holy Ghost which is given unto us, (Romans 5:5). It was easy to love Ms. M, although I experienced pain, frustration, and other negative emotions. The good days outweighed the bad days, during my time caring for her. If I had to, I would do it all again.

My journey continues because I'm yet in the land of the living, and I am grateful to God for every opportunity given to me to show someone love.

CHAPTER 8

The Journey to Transition

A s I rode in the transport vehicle taking my mom home from the hospital, I realized that would be the last trip we would take home from the hospital, rehabilitation facility, and nursing home visits and stays. The reality hit me as I reflected on what had occurred with her over the past two weeks. *Let him who walks in the dark, who has no light, trust in the name of the Lord and rely on his God,* **Isaiah 50:10 (NIV).**

Mom had been having chest congestion accompanied by a cough that showed no signs of improving. I knew it would be a challenge getting her out of the bed, dressed, down the steps, into a wheelchair, and into a vehicle to transport her to medical care, because she was weak and had very little mobility. So, I had to decide whether to take her to the hospital or urgent care. After weighing the pros and cons and projecting the what if scenarios, I decided to take her to Kaiser's twenty-four-hour Urgent Care (UC) which offered temporary hospital-like care and rooms. My logic was if she needed more care, they would take care of her until they transferred her to a Kaiser Hospital.

I am with you and will watch over you wherever you go, **Genesis 28:15 (NIV).** Leading up to this UC visit, things had begun to shift. Mom's appetite significantly changed. She was eating much less and was having problems swallowing. The UC doctor diagnosis included pneumonia, urinary tract infection, and dehydration. When they decided to transfer her to Washington Hospital Center, I knew from previous experiences, I would be up for several hours without rest. So, I went home to pack some items I would need for the journey, which was just beginning. Little did I know it would ultimately be the beginning of mom's transition.

Give your worries to the Lord and he will take care of you, **Psalm 55:22 (NCV).** During our last visit in the hospital, I remembered mom breaking out in song while my sister and I were sitting in her room. The song was *"Come by Here Lord."* I joined mom in singing that song. Knowing how much she loved to listen to music, I used my cell phone to play songs from one of my playlists. It was evident she was enjoying the music which included gospel, soothing instrumental sounds, rhythm and blues, classical, jazz, and meditation. Later, she began to sing *"Goin' Up Yonder."* A day or so later, we were told that her dementia, a preexisting condition, had advanced, and we should make plans to put her in hospice care. The options were to put her in a facility or take her home. At this point and stage in her care at home, we had a team of caregivers who had loved her and been caring for her for some time. They were a blessing-a gift from God. So, the decision was easy-a no-brainer. She would return home. At that point, we did not know if she would be with us for hours, days, weeks, months, or a couple of years. Yet God knew and had a plan. A hospice agency was selected and additional care including equipment was ordered to arrive before mom returned home. During mom's short stay in the hospital, she had become even more frail. Her ability to swallow. diminished significantly. She was less responsive and sleeping a lot more. It was difficult to see and hear her groan in pain. Because she did not have enough fat to cushion her body, lying in bed became uncomfortable. Therefore, making sure she was turned on a regular basis became one of our main priorities.

Rest in the Lord and wait patiently for Him, **Psalm 37:7 (NKJV).** Once we were informed by the hospital mom needed to be in hospice care, discharge plans were made to return her home. We arranged for transport services that would take her from hospital bed on a stretcher to home hospital bed. The plan was for me to ride home with mom and Janice, one of mom's home health aides and caregivers, would meet us at mom's house. During that drive from the hospital to mom's home, I spoke lovingly to her before she finally drifted to sleep. As I rode in the vehicle, I began to reflect on the last week, including the songs she had sung. It was in that moment, I realized she knew her time on earth was coming to an end soon and very soon. The reality hit me that this trip home would be our last together and unlike those before. I prayed, meditated, and played light music. As tears began to flow, my heart began to ache and break. My mommy was preparing to go home to be with our Lord. As a believer in Christ, it was a bitter-sweet moment.

Even though I walk through the darkest valley, I will fear no evil, for you are with me; your rod and your staff they comfort me, **Psalm 23:4 (NIV).** Accepting the fact that mom was declining led me to think of things which could be done to make the best of mom's last days on earth. Of course, the basics came to mind: surround her with people who loved her, contact and invite family and friends to visit, love her up, give her the best care possible, make all efforts to keep her comfortable, etc. When we broke the news to Angeline, Lucy, Janice, Betty, and Clarice, her caregivers, sadness overtook them. They too loved mom. As I began to focus on what else could be done to bring joy to mom in her current state, the gift of music came to mind. I had started making a playlist for mom during her hospital stay. So, the first night home, I added many more songs to the playlist. When I finished, there were 12 hours of music. We purchased a tablet and stereo headphones for her to listen to the playlist. Every day her home health aides would put on the headphones and let mom listen to her playlist continuously. We knew she enjoyed the music because she would tap her toes to the beat of the music.

Satisfy us in the morning with your unfailing love, that we may sing for joy and be glad all our days, **Psalm 90:14 (NIV).** Sometimes when I visited mom, I would play the music through the speakers and sing and dance for her. She would look at me, shake her head, and smile as she often did when I "performed" for her. I made sure to talk to her during my visits as well. I didn't want her sitting in silence when the music was not playing, so I asked the caregivers and other visitors to talk to her about positive news, weather, their lives and family, and the loved ones in pictures posted around her room. It was also important to me that mom was touched. I am naturally touchy feely, and I know touch is a sense that communicates and can bring joy, comfort, and healing in ways not seen. To show my affection, I always gave mom hugs and held her hands, kissed her on her forehead and cheeks, and massaged her hands and feet.

Though Mom began to sleep more and eat less, she still enjoyed listening to her music, as evidenced by her foot movement. It brought us joy to see this because we were limited in what we could do for her, except make sure she was comfortable. I began to stay overnight to help care for mom. Every day, I was on the phone with the hospice agency inquiring about what we could do to make her comfortable and get nutrition in her. About two days before mom went home to be with our Lord, signs she was nearing her transition began. She would not take any nutrition even though we were using droppers to administer liquids orally. The information provided by hospice about the signs to watch were helpful.

On the morning of April 17, mom did not open her eyes and acknowledge me or Clarice, her daytime aide. I contacted the hospice nurse and my sisters with an update, indicating that the time was near. I texted Minister Hooper from my church and asked him to call and pray. I put the phone on speaker as he prayed. Mom still did not open her eyes. The hospice nurse arrived and examined mom. I let her know I had contacted my sisters, and they were on their way. She asked to speak with us, downstairs, when they arrived. In the meantime, I sat by the bed and held my mommy's hand as she listened to her music through her stereo headphones. Then, the Holy Spirit told me to remove the headphones and put the music on speaker. First, I played and sang *"Come by Here Lord"* followed by *"A Song for Momma"* by Boyz II Men. I switched up the lyrics to make it more personal as I sang the song to her from my heart and held her hands. She did not respond in any way. Though she was faintly breathing, I knew she could hear me. Mom still had not opened her eyes. The next song on the playlist was *"Going Up Yonder."* As I began to sing that song, the Spirit began to stir in me, and there was movement in the atmosphere.

Mom, for the first time that morning, opened her eyes as I sang to her. I stopped singing and said to her "Mommy, we will always love you, and we will be okay. It is okay for you to leave us on earth, to go to your heavenly home, and to rest. Thank you for all the memories, love and care you gave us." Then, she raised up, looked me in my eyes lovingly, and took her last breath. Being there to see my mommy as she made her transition was bittersweet. I was so grateful that God allowed it to happen the way it did. I could not have planned a more beautiful transition and farewell. This gift was divine and intended especially for me. I can never thank God enough! Shortly thereafter, my sisters, nieces, and nephews arrived. In the days following, I reflected on the past few years. After I had a stroke and came home from rehabilitation, my mom helped care for me. She prepared meals and took me to medical appointments. About a year later, her life changed. She was hospitalized and the unexpected happened. During that stay, we were informed she could no longer live alone. Either someone had to be in the house around the clock or we would have to put her in a nursing home. At that moment, our family life changed dramatically. It was a shock! What would we do? Decisions had to be made quickly, but we were not ready to make them.

Confronted with overwhelming information and major decisions to make, we were unprepared intellectually, emotionally, and financially. I was still recovering from the stroke. My sisters were working. We did not have much experience with caregiving, except for providing care for my father 25 years prior. I remembered going to the Lord in prayer seeking help, answers, and direction. Prayer became a bigger part of my routine and way of living after the stroke. God answered quickly!!! My nephew and family were facing homelessness. The owner of the house for which they were paying rent, notified them that he was facing foreclosure, and they had to move. very soon. The option of the grandchildren moving in with mom, became a win-win for the family. But we had to act very quickly to prepare the house to accommodate four additional family members. That was the beginning of our caregiving journey. In the years following, we made major adjustments and experienced unmeasurable stress in how we lived.

I love the Lord because he hears my prayers and answers them. Because he bends down and listens, I will pray for as long as I breathe, **Psalm 116:1 (TLB)**. It was a gift from our Creator to have my nephew, niece and grand niece and nephew living with mom. This bought us a little time to figure out the next steps which involved bringing aides and. caregivers into the home to help care for mom. Life and independence as mom knew it changed. There were major adjustments made and the paradigm shifted. She could no longer prepare meals and drive but was still mobile with a little help from a cane or walker.

Thankfully, the level of care mom needed at this stage was low. In time, it would grow. My sisters were able to get mom into a program in which she received a caregiver who assisted her with daily tasks and accompanied her to scheduled appointments and weekly visits to a senior center that provided activity and social interaction. The added blessing was that we did not have to pay for it. Programs and services for seniors vary by state or city. It was a huge blessing for us that the District of Columbia is a city that takes care of its seniors, thanks in part to the mayor at that time who now rests in peace. As time went on, caregiving needs increased. Over the next year or two, the number of caregivers we went through were numerous due to poor work ethics, negative attitudes, inconsistencies, and communication barriers. It was draining, physically and emotionally.

Love is patient. Love is kind, 1 **Corinthians 13:4 (NIV).** Over the years, we experienced a myriad of situations, inconveniences, changes in personality, rehabilitation, resentment, mood swings, personal struggles, challenges, cognitive changes, disagreements, hospital stays and impositions. We could write a book on caregiving for loved ones. But, no matter what, our goal and objectives were always to keep mom aging at home with love and dignity. She had communicated this wish many years before (to never be put in an institution), and it was a promise my sisters made to my father. In time, the challenges had me reconsidering whether this was possible. Yet God carried us through even the most difficult times.

The Lord gives strength to His people; the Lord will bless His people with peace, **Psalm 29:11, (NKJV).** For a few years, Matt, Olivia, Mateo, and Brishe' (grands and great grands) lived with and cared for mom. Our village was taking care of our matriarch. It was nice to see how protective and loving they were with their grandmother. Each grand and great grand grew to have a special relationship with her and an even stronger bond before they eventually moved out. When we received advance notice from Matt and Olivia that they would be moving after much deliberation and mixed feelings, it was one we understood. During their time living with mom, Olivia had an accident at work which changed her life and that of our family. Again, we experienced trials, tribulations, challenges, and unexpected major adjustments. When facing challenges and difficult times, *God will not leave you but will walk with you during the difficulties and guide your steps* - **Genesis 50:20 (NIV)**.

We rejoice in our sufferings, knowing that our suffering produces endurance, and endurance produces character, and character produces hope, **Romans 5:3-4. (ESV).** My faith was elevated after the stroke. So, I did not worry when mom became ill, but prayed instead. I had peace because I knew God would take care of mom, her needs, and our family, and that was my daily prayer. He knew our situation and circumstances.

God says, I will be with you. I will not leave you or forsake you, **Joshua 1:5. (ESV).** God showed up again, lighting our path to the next chapter. We began to look at how we would fill the gap and the need when Matt and Olivia moved. Carol, my oldest sister, came across the concept of "house sharing" which we pursued by casting a search among our inner circles and community. Lucy was identified from a religious circle and vetted. We entered into a house share agreement. Lucy, who moved in, provided an overnight presence in the home and helped care for mom, along with the day-to-day caregivers until mom's passing. The fulfillment of God's promise depends entirely on trusting God and his way, and then simply embracing him and what he does.

God's promise arrives as a pure gift, **Romans 4:16, (The Message)**. At the end of mom's transition to Glory, we are grateful to have had the privilege of honoring and serving her in her later years. When she left this earth, all that we went through was worth it. There were no regrets or resentment. Joy intertwined with missing her physical presence is what we feel as we each go through our own stages of grief. Caregiving is one of the greatest acts of love one can give to their loved one. And, faith, trusting in a Higher Power, and prayers, both personal and intercessory, got us through it all.

When all is said and done, the last word is Immanuel – *God-With-Us,* **Isaiah 8:10, (The Message)**.

CHAPTER 9

A Caregiver's Journey of the Soul

My life was forever impacted. My mother – my confidant, my earthly anchor...the words that were being echoed, were now faded, hollow, yet profound in tone. When I heard the diagnosis from the ER doctor say – 'It's her heart.' Congestive heart failure, the diagnosis in which I grew to learn, and what I entailed hours later, would forever change my mother's world and how she knew and live it. Major restrictions were coming her way. Hearing the diagnosis and the specifics for the next couple of hours, affected me tremendously that I became weak, faint, and feeling I was going to become the next patient.

Instead, I pulled myself together, put on that stoic-brave face, as her doctors muffled what sounded to me like unintelligible jargon, like the infamous teacher of the cartoon character, Charlie Brown. Her voice resonated initially as a hollow irritating echo because I was too distracted with other competing voices that were screaming in my ears. "Your mother is going to die from this!! You can't handle this!! You're too weak." And there I was becoming agitated by the moment! I needed God to fix this! And now! My mother dearest, OMG! It's her heart! And so, it started with congestive heart failure. And almost a year of rehabilitation for my mother, would bring a strategic health regime – diet, moderate physical activity, she was going to need on-going assistance maintaining her health and the internal and external factors that come with her new lifestyle.

I had now become primary overseer for the woman who had not only nurtured our family's health, but also as a registered nurse as she was would have to put her life into others' hands on a long-term basis. She became depressed about it and who could blame her? She began to have cognitive-therapy and drug-therapy to help her cope with this "new" normal and she continued throughout her life to have to not only deal with her challenging emotional, social and cognitive health compromised because of her physical health, but this new self-help development from her family was really going to take it to another level. Years later, twenty years to be exact, my mother's health index had plummeted from major to severe, as well as my life-trajectory of wife, mother, and student. I tirelessly worked toward receiving my second degree – in which I am still working toward to this day, all the while in the process of trying to keep my own health in-check because declining health was quickly taking a toll.

Every aspect of my life as I knew it and had become accustomed to, was now surreal as if I was living out of my body and could not phantom it being my "new" normal. I became angry, resentful, and guilty for thinking of how this was going to change my comfortable life. And I don't mean a twinge of these emotions, but a lot... Then another fast ball hit me! In 2011, I became terribly ill. I was rushed to the hospital where I was diagnosed with Graves' Disease. It felt like the tunnel of doom was closing in, and there was no way I would be able to stay afloat with this health crisis and be an effective caregiver. Why? I asked myself. Why was I undergoing all this stress all at once?

As the caregiver responsibilities grew over the years, so did the enormous guilt. I had my own family – a husband and sons. I felt horrible that I was failing my sons. A mother who shifted a lot of the parental responsibilities willingly over to my supportive husband, who thankfully took on the role of dual parenting, literally picked up the slack. I will forever be thankful that he supported me in parenting, caregiving and assisting with my mother and father. My life for hers hasn't been a bed of healthy-blossoming roses...it has been some thorns in between...but I prayed diligently – for God's will for my mother's well-being and for "me." I began feeling whole again in 2019, when I attended a women's empowerment event, hosted by my cousin. Unapologetically "Me." One of the activities, there that really was profound for me was when we were given a piece of paper and pen to privately write down what we wanted to discard – let go of and feel free about doing so. There was a shredder that women then could shred their list of what were their insecurities and what they wanted to be freed from the guilt that was still weighing them down. It felt so liberating. On my list, I expressed how guilt for wanting time for myself – for Tonya, and for Tonya only.

This is my soul-to-soul story of encouragement to caregivers whom by chance or even by intention, will turn to this chapter and draw even a dose of strength, confidence, and perseverance to keep the faith in their soul-walk journey. I say a dose, because it's a journey and every ounce of strength can make impact in the input of the outcome... Please, caregivers of the present, and/the future, please as I am writing this, tears are streaming from my eyes because it is vitally important: Do not lose the "You" in the journey. My Mother Dearest transitioned to glory on a Sunday, April 19 th , 2020.

Although she is not here with me on earth, she continues to cover me - her affirmations of strength I can hear clearly in a gentle whispering –'Sweet daughter I want you to continue living your God-given purpose.'

I am Tonya Rivers and I'm praying for you!

CHAPTER 10

My Life for His Life

As a wife and caregiver, these two scriptures are conceivable through Faith in Christ: **Proverbs 18:22** - *He who finds a wife finds a good thing and obtains favor from the Lord* and **John 15:13** - *Greater love hath no man than this that he lay down his life for his friends.*

I, Ms. Vivian J. Smallwood, through the greatest action of God's love, gave my life, as a caregiver, for my late husband, Mr. John Kenneth (Kenny) Smallwood. Scripture narrates that the greatest love shown was demonstrated through Christ Jesus - His love for humanity - respectively;

"For God so loved the world that He gave His only begotten Son, that whosoever believe in Him should not

perish but, have everlasting life" (John 3:16).

In November 2008, the love of my life, Kenny was admitted to the hospital for removal of polyps from his colon. The procedure could not be performed in a local doctor's office because the polyps were next to an artery. He remained in the hospital after the surgery and was released to go home three days later. After being home for about a day, Kenny began having a few complications, so back to the hospital (emergency room) we went. The ER doctor suspected that there was a possible blockage and re-admitted Kenny to the hospital. As we were going to the Intensive Care Unit (ICU), Kenny and I were talking, and he was already anticipating going home. When we arrived in the ICU area, the nurse asked if I could step out while they prepped him, checked his blood pressure, and a host of other ICU check-in protocols.

After about a half hour, I began to wonder what was taking them so long to get him prepped. As I approached the nurses' station to inquire, I heard a "Code Blue" alert come across the intercom. I did not pay attention to the alert. My daughters, Qawana and Reseda, heard the alert, inquired, and was advised that it was Kenny. They found me and tried to keep me from going into the room, but the Holy Spirit led me to be with my husband. I was startled as I entered Kenny's room to see all hell breaking loose. There was a crowd of doctors and nurses surrounding his bed. I immediately made my way to his bedside, where he was being intubated. Tears were streaming out of his eyes, and his face was swollen larger than ever. I screamed, "What happened? What happened? He was talking, breathing, and making jokes when I left the room! What happened?" No one could answer my question. I immediately began to pray in the Spirit, while spitting and sputtering, with tears streaming down my face. The head nurse came over to console me, but still, no one could provide a definitive answer as to what happened. By continuing to question the medical staff about what happened to Kenny, wasn't as much of a concern as ensuring he was still alive. Numbness fell over my entire thought process. His eyes were closed. He was lying in the bed like a zombie on a ventilator and placed in a medically induced coma.

My daughters, other family members, friends and a few people from church came. They began to pray for

Kenny, as they were shocked at what they saw. I remember vividly, the feeling of loss and despair. The shock factor for me felt like a piercing in my heart that left me asking, "Is this really happening?" About two days passed, and it was suggested that I should go home for a couple of hours, shower, and refresh. So, I agreed, only because I knew that my daughters would be there with Kenny until I returned. Still dazed, and confused, scared, and heartbroken, I left the hospital to go home, but when I came to myself, I was sitting on the dirty floor in the corner of the men's department in Walmart. People strolled through the area of the store as if I wasn't there. They probably thought I was a homeless person on drugs. Tears were rolling down my face, and I was crying for God's help. Yet no one came to ask if I was okay. Even if they had, they would not have understood, because I didn't. Finally, an hour had passed, and my daughters called to check on me and let me know that there was no change with Kenny. By this time, I was at home. I had showered and was leaving. the house headed back to the hospital. Still in a daze thinking this was a dream and not really happening, but at the same time, aware that this incident was real.

Kenny had been in an induced coma for about 30 days. He could not be left alone because he was heavily sedated with various complications, any one of which could have been fatal. So, I was there 24/7, except twice a week when I went home to shower and change clothes. While at the hospital, I had a bag with clothes, soap, towels, face cloths, and other necessities. The nurses provided toothbrushes, sheets, blankets, and anything else to make me comfortable. The doctors would, at times, ensure a cart was set-up in the waiting room with entrees, salads, dessert, soda, water and juice for family and friends. I was greatly appreciative, but still distraught and yet hopeful. Kenny was still in an induced coma in December 2008. I was still there, around the clock, as his caregiver. The doctors decided that it was necessary to take Kenny out of the induced coma later in the month. They believed he would be in a vegetative state, but I discerned differently. It was important to be by my husband's side and pray continuously in the Spirit. I thank God for the nurses and doctors who knew that my presence was necessary, as the power of God's Spirit was in the midst. I had faith that all would be well.

The doctors stopped the drug, Propofol, used for medically induced comas, but Kenny remained comatose. At times, I would see him move his legs, his eyeballs (through his eyelids), and even. wiggle; so, I knew he was still fighting to live. The neurologist thought I was delirious. They wanted to admit me because they thought I was losing it. They offered me sedatives, but I refused. In January 2009, Kenny was diagnosed with having a stroke throughout his brain (on both sides, front, and back). In short, he had a severe hemorrhage in the brain's left and right hemispheres. He was still in an unconscious state. "My life for his life" became more apparent because if I had not consistently been involved in his care, 24/7, Kenny would have died, especially with the lack of hospital staff. I had seen more code blues, with people deceasing due to understaffing, the limited experience of CNAs and RNs, and the absence of the patient's loved ones. This was disheartening and stressful, but I remained prayerful. The following dates are a few of the "My Life for His Life" journaling notes recorded during Kenny's journey from January 2009 through February 10, 2010.

January 6, 2009 – another day that I continued to thank God for better, as I walked by faith. The nurse on staff did not know how to suction the trachea (she suctioned up blood), nor did she know how to take a rectal temperature. I literally took the nurse by the hand and escorted her out

of Kenny's room, and called the lead male nurse to aid and assist. I took my husband's rectal temperature around 4 a.m. and it was 102.8. Medicine was given immediately to avoid any unnecessary complications. By this time, I had no sleep, and was tired, but God's strength remained greater.

January 28, 2009 – I prayed for God's perfect will and healing for Kenny-to God be the glory!

January 30, 2009 – I prayed for God to breathe a breath of fresh air into Kenny's spirit to restore him to the original design created.

January 31, 2009 – Today's daily journal: "All sacrifice and all suffering is redemptive: to teach the individual or to be used to raise and help others. Nothing is by chance. Divine Mind, and its wonder working, is beyond my finite mind to understand. No detail is forgotten in God's Plans, already perfect" (God's Calling Journal). The scripture that resonated with me was Jeremiah 29:11-*For I know the plans I have for you, "declares the Lord," plans to prosper you and not to harm you, plans to give you hope and a future.* Praise God, for all was well, and I continued to walk by faith, as I believed that we would receive God's promises. We were believers waiting on a mighty move of God. I believed Kenny would be restored.

February 1, 2009 – I woke up to another day where I washed my face, brushed my teeth, got dressed and woke Kenny up for his day. He was very agitated, but I continued to take care of him. I began praying that he was walking by faith and not by sight. I remained steadfast in my faith and refused to lose my joy. I knew God was still with us, as we were one in Christ-together for God's glory.

Although Kenny still had the trachea to aid in his breathing, he began showing signs of life. The trachea was a challenge within itself. I thank God that I understood what it meant for my life to become his life. God guided me with His Spirit in my weakness. It was time for the trachea to be capped with a Passy Muir Valve. I was so nervous because I wasn't sure he'd be able to breathe on his own. If not, he would surely die. This was an attack of the enemy playing on my faith. I rebuked those thoughts and prayed for God to intervene. The trachea was capped, and the journey to restoration continued. I remember vividly how Kenny would tightly hold my hand and didn't want me to leave his eyesight. He knew he could not care for himself or articulate his thoughts. Remember, he had a serious stroke-a severe hemorrhage in the brain's left and right hemispheres. Caring for Kenny was surreal, as I witnessed him, a 68-year-old, 6 feet 2 inches tall, 250-pound man, become an infant within his body. I was the caregiver, but God was the cure-giver. God's strength became my strength, and He was always there to lift me up when I was weary.

Most people did not understand what we were going through. Kenny would always say, "Babe, it is you and I in this life together. Don't worry about anyone else. God has you." So, I forgave our family, friends and even those who did not care because they did not understand. Even if they did, I chose to forgive them anyway. Kenny's team of doctors recommended that he be transferred to a hospital for acute stroke. rehabilitation. It was common knowledge that a stroke patient's recovery had to begin three months after the onset of the stroke. So, Kenny was moved to Lady of Lourdes-Camden on February 2, 2009. I remember his first movable action. He blew me a kiss with his lips puckered and a distorted frown on his face, prior to leaving Rancocas Valley Hospital in Willingboro, New Jersey. Reseda and I laughed and hoped for Kenny's rehabilitation to be a positive step on his journey to recovery.

Another moment of hope - I pulled Kenny's wallet out of my purse and in his stroke associated voice, he said, "That's my wallet-where's my money?" We rejoiced with laughter because he had not only spoken, but also remembered. The hospital staff at Lady of Lourdes-Camden had us in the same room, with my bed next to his, for the duration of his acute rehabilitation.

February 8, 2009 – I was awakened by the call of my husband. He was cold, and he could not recall how to cover himself. I covered him both naturally and spiritually through prayer. I thanked God for continuously allowing His Spirit to lead, guide and strengthen me as I cared for my husband. I would cry out, , "Lord, please continue to use me for your glory and to be that helpmate for my husband, your son. I know that even during the trials and tribulations, as long as I am faithful, you will restore the time lost to me. I thank you for opening the eyes of my heart Lord, for Godly wisdom. I will continue to be steadfast in servitude, as I minister to my husband, *"The steps of a good man (woman) are ordered by the Lord: and he (she) delight in His way* (Psalm 37:23).

We finally left Lady of Lourdes Hospital and went home in April 2009. Yet rehabilitation did not stop. Intensive neurological therapy continued. Outpatient, and home health care was administered for speech, cognitive, physical, and occupational therapy. Kenny also came homewith a feeding tube, and I was responsible for feeding him. Kenny slept a lot, which was good because rest was noted as a major factor in healing. However, I did not sleep. Kenny's care required me to be available 24/7. Continuous prayers and believing that he would regain his life as intended by God, became my reality. Kenny's health was partially restored. He regained about 70% of his normal functions. But he still suffered from memory loss and other impairments. He was considered right-sided hemiplegic.

In November 2009, I became ill and was admitted to the hospital for three days. As I gave my life for his life, I no longer practiced self-care. However, self-care is important for a caregiver, as you can't pour from an empty cup. Reseda volunteered to take care of Kenny during my hospital stay. When I came home, I decided that I needed help. So, a certified nursing assistant was scheduled to assist me in providing care for Kenny. Kenny would always want to talk in the wee hours of the night/early morning. Even though I was tired and needed rest, I was there to listen. I am so happy that I did. God's word encouraged strength as a wife, a friend and as a Caregiver: **Isaiah 40:31**, *"But those who hope in the Lord will renew their strength. They will soar on wings like eagles; they will run and not grow weary; they will walk and not be faint"*.

The doctors indicated that a stroke could take five to ten years for recovery. We were thankful to God that Kenny's recovery began within four months of his stroke diagnosis. However, in December 2009, he was stricken with Agent Orange from serving in Vietnam. This was a very critical moment of his life for he was now diagnosed with Leiomyosarcoma, an incurable soft tissue cancer within the shoulder that metastasized to his lungs within two months. This illness presented other debilitating issues not only for him, but also for my role as a caregiver, which will be shared at another time.

All in all, Kenny was tired, and his physical life ended February 10, 2010, but his spiritual life ascended with God. The life after his death is still a part of the life that I am living now through the memories as his wife and his caregiver. It is by God's mercy and grace that I have made it this far by faith. There were times when the thought "I cannot hold on any longer" resonated, but the memories, the prayers and God's sustaining voice have lifted me- *not by might, nor by power, but by His Spirit* (**Zechariah 4:6**).

Before closing this chapter, I'd like to thank those whose names were not mentioned, due tonot having approval or permission for publishing their name in this Anthology. But, if you happen to purchase this book and read this short chapter, I am sure that you will know who you are and realize the appreciation resonating in my heart for the love shown. I thank you and praise God, for even in death, "We Win". Also, please note, the neurologist who facilitated the care of my husband recommended a book, "My Stroke of Insight" by Jill Bolte Taylor, Ph.D., a trained brain scientist, who experienced a massive stroke.

This book shares her perspective on the brain and its capacity for recovery. The information presents knowledge of how the brain works and imparts teachings that can be used as a recovery guide for brain injury. My Stroke of Insight tremendously provided insightful information and awareness on how to care for a person diagnosed with a brain hemorrhage. This book was very instrumental in caring for my husband and teaching how to care for people who suffer from such a debilitating illness.

I have learned what it means to be a caregiver through the many tasks that God has given me. *"My Life for His Life"* acknowledges my "ministry of presence" as a way of being available to people and listening for the call that focuses on caregiving in the lives of other-To God be the glory! I will leave the ninety-nine for the one- **Matthew 18:12-14** *" What do you think? If a man has a hundred sheep, and one of them gets lost, will he not leave the ninety -nine on the mountain and go in search of the one* *that is lost? And if it turns out that he finds it, I assure you and most solemnly say to you, he rejoices over it more than over the ninety-nine that did not get lost.*

So, it is not the will of your Father who is in heaven that one of these little ones be lost." Agape Love and Blessings-forevermore!

CHAPTER 11

Learning to Depend on God

As I began to take care of my daughter, Maulika, I realized that I would have to figure out a lot on my own. The medical world had failed her. They didn't know what to do with her. They had never seen a child in her condition. Maulika had special needs. She was born with her brain outside of her head. I had to carry her with her head in my hand and her brain on my forearm. She could not talk. She was blind and fed with a machine. She also wore diapers. I had to do everything for her, and in the beginning, it was a tough process. Over the years, however, I learned to enjoy caring for her. I prayed over her and played music that she loved. I knew it was keeping her comfortable and keeping her alive.

Maulika showed me that she needed different things. She could not talk, she was blind and she was fed with a machine. Her diapers had to be changed. I had to do everything for her, and in the beginning, it was a process. But over the years, I learned to enjoy doing it. I knew it was keeping this human being comfortable. I knew it was keeping her alive. I learned to pray over her. She loved music. So, I learned to experiment with different music. I learned so much during that time about caregiving for people. I also learned that I had to care for myself also. They did not give her a long time to live. They said she would live no longer than a month. Yet she had lived three months. I took her to get shots, and the doctor refused to give her the shots. He said she didn't need them. That was the first time in my life I ever wanted to put my hands on another human being. I was so angry because I knew they were not looking at Maulika like a human being. I had to do something.

I prayed fervently because I was depressed. Then, I looked up scriptures and **Deuteronomy 31:8** *"The LORD himself goes before you and will be with* *you; he will never leave you nor forsake you. Do not be afraid; do not be discouraged"* stuck out to me. I meditated on the scripture over and over. I would get up in the morning, pray, do my devotion and sometimes, write in my journal. I bought several journals. I used one to write prayers and another to write about Maulika.

Caregiving is an experience that everybody should share. Being a caregiver will bring everything out of you. It will teach you about you. It will bring you closer to God if nothing else will. And during the time that you're caregiving, you must keep in touch with yourself. I've lost myself for a little while, but I found myself. I was so stressed and depressed that I gained 80 pounds. I didn't have the energy I needed to take care of 10 children, so I had to do something to lose weight. So, I started the Weight Watcher's diet. I journaled about this also.

God gave me almost 16 years with Maulika. Sometimes I would wonder how I would get through the tough times. What was I doing? I must've been crazy to take on such a great responsibility! No, I wasn't crazy. I loved my daughter so much that I eventually began to love what I was doing for her. When she died, everyone predicted that I would die too. They did not expect me to make it through the loss, but I did because I knew that's what I was supposed to do. I advise all caregivers to stay in prayer, stay in scripture, get out, go out to eat, walk, run, be in church, and continue to be social. *"I shall not die but live and declare the works of the Lord."* **Psalms 1:18**.

After her death, I've gone on to write books, speak publically, prepare for a radio show, and I'm going to pastor a church again. God is so amazing because He showed me time and time again to do as He says and don't make up my own thing, but to lean on Jesus.

There's a song that I used to sing as a child and I didn't understand it then, but I understand it so much now. I learned how to lean and depend on Jesus, for I found out that if I trust Him, he will provide.

CHAPTER 12

Endless Love

It's Not a Feeling. It's a Verb... Faith is the key

This is dedicated to my circle of family and friends who kept me lifted in prayer during a few challenging seasons when my faith was being tested. Thank you for your sweet compassion and continuous support that always reminded me of the goodness of the Lord. Things happen in our lives that are not fair, and we have a choice to live a bitter life or believe for a better one. We can unlock our faith and trust that God has a plan, and He has everything under control. As a child, I remember singing *"He's Got the Whole World in His Hand"* (based on Psalms 95:4) and thinking WOW! There is like a "kabillion" people on earth, the hand of God must be H-U-G-E! Whether I am in the saddest of valleys, flying high as a kite, or desperate in the depths of the sea, God can reach me.

An excerpt from one of my personal Facebook "Request for prayer" post:

I only know one thing to do when a trial hits, and that is pray without ceasing. We are challenged today, not to believe the enemies report. My husband has been diagnosed for the second time with several masses on his spine. They have caused nerve damage and great pain. We are locating the best surgeons now, as he will need immediate surgery. But we are believing God's good report that says, He will never leave us or forsake us! This is an all-day procedure and we know the Master Surgeon is always on duty and through Him, ALL THINGS ARE POSSIBLE. I ask you to join me in praying these scriptures over my best friend and humble husband.

> *We believe this prayer, offered in faith, will put Him back on his feet.* (James 5:15)
>
> *God will restore him to good health, only He can cure the incurable.* (Jeremiah 30:17)
>
> *God is our source of strength; the calm before the storm; protect him and our family.* (Psalms 46:1)

It is our prayer that no weapon formed against him shall prosper. (**Isaiah 54:17**)

Lord, we ask for strength, endurance, microscopic eyes, and skillful hands for his operating team. Father, we are watching, praying and grateful that you hear and answer our request. Your will be done.

In Jesus Name, AMEN-

No greater love

Even before the surgery began, I was already shifting gears. I went from a crazy in love wife and incredibly busy mother of four boys; to an overprotective patient advocate and stressed woman, trying to keep the train on the track. Fighting for my husband's needs became a priority. After all, his life was at stake. His recovery hangs on getting what he needs when he needs it. So, if I do not look out for him, who will? There is a lot to manage and time is of the essence when decisions must be made about his care.

My plate was already full. So I was overwhelmed when the hospital staff began spouting out the details for the financial responsibility and payment plans, the insurance coverage and explanations, the combinations of medicines and side effects, the surgical success rate and daunting risk, our legal rights and medical resources available, and oh how they carried on. As a home-maker I was providing around the clock care for my children, while performing most of the household duties. So, adding the full load of my sweetheart and taking on a sudden increase in responsibilities did not leave much time for me. So, I kept moving items from my to-do-list to the next day. Twenty-four hours just was not enough! I would say to myself, "If it was important today; it'll be real important tomorrow" and just maybe, I can cross some things off. I used to pray for more hours or that the Lord would not allow the time to pass so fast so I could accomplish my task.

I am not one to buckle under stress, but there was a lot to process. Health care is not my specialty, so I had to learn quickly. After a successful surgery, he resided at Magee Rehabilitation Hospital for a few months. It was difficult to see him in a vulnerable position, but there was not time for me to pity him. I had to prepare because I had become a full-time caregiver.

There's no greater love than putting someone else's needs ahead of your own. (John 15:13) It's not often a desired choice to sacrifice your life for another. Consider

105

how many mothers would throw themselves in front of a speeding bullet or car to save their child's life? That is exactly what caregiving requires; laying down my life for someone else's. That is exactly what I meant when I vowed in sickness and in health.

I know my husband loves me unconditionally and endlessly. Sometimes I wonder if the tables were turned, would he do the same for me? Would he hire someone? Would he leave me in a facility with round-the-clock assistance? Would he give up everything, even his job, to take care of me? Would he wipe my crevices after I soiled myself? What about changing my bandages and treating my bed sores? Would he try and cook my favorite meals and serve me in bed daily? Could he give me a sponge bath and style my hair? How would he manage the schedule of appointments for the kids and me? Would he tend to my every need all-day-long after caring for the boys? Could he bear to give me shots? How much sleep would he be willing to lose while keeping an eye and ear tuned on me? I do believe he would do his absolute best to care for me.

Unselfishness is necessary as a caregiver because my

needs must take a back seat. This is the picture of love in its purest form.

Colossians 3:14-5 tells me to wrap myself in love and let God's peace control my heart when unsettling circumstances arise.

If you think you're lonely now

There have been times when my house was full of people and I felt empty or isolated by the circumstances. Although family visited for emotional support, neighbors generously provided off lunch and dinner, friends picked up the kids from practice (and politely tried not to pry), pastors prayed with us, yet no amount of connection could fill the giant hole in my heart. This was a very demnanding solo gig.

My husband was my listening ear. So, I felt a sense of loneliness during this time because he was no longer emotionally available for what I was going through, and I didn't want to burden him. But who would I trust to confide in? These would be delicate conversations, involving sensitive details and others won't be able to relate. Who am I kidding? Some of its just embarrassing. I didn't hold that against him because he's not responsible for what happened to him. As a Christian, It's our job to do the best we can and give the consequences to God. The circumstances are beyond my hubby's control. I know he is dealing with a lot, so I don't burden him with my moments of loneliness.

I'm sure that sounds sad but who was I to talk to? I didn't want to share intimate challenges with my mother, that's gross! And his mother would be trying to come over and help her first-born, which would have been totally embarrassing for him. We shared great friendships with our siblings, but they were dealing with their own family issues. Plus, all the above loved ones were out of town. These are not easy conversations to have in-person, let alone on the phone. Plus, there was a bigger concern with privacy. You can't be putting your spouse's business out there. No one needs to know some of that stuff. Now, if he shares it, that's ok. I couldn't find the words to describe the constant demand of my new role. So, I felt as if no one understood what I had to go through all day and all night. It was something that had to be experienced, but I don't believe people really want to understand the plight of a caregiver.

They're just being kind by asking. "Is everything ok? Do you need anything? How's it going? Is he getting any better?" What I was feeling and hoping, was that he needs to get better. I hope I don't appear bitter and resentful towards him. I need some time to rest and doing nothing for no one.

The voice of truth

I couldn't believe what I was hearing. Why Lord? Why him again? It had been seven years since his second spinal surgery (and 16 years since his first surgery), and we had to prepare for a third. After the surgery, he was shut up at Magee again. My frustrated and scared spouse said that he was ready to check out of rehab. He was ready to leave earlier than the doctors recommended, saying that the hospital was no place for sick people. I understood what he meant, but we had great insurance so I thought he should have stayed and gotten his money's worth. However, I knew that rehab was a very humbling and depressing experience for many. Therefore, I wasn't surprised when he thought he would recover better at home with his family. Yet I couldn't help but think what that meant for me. Rehab can be very depressing and very humbling; many patients are hopeless about their circumstances, lack of abilities and bleak future. From his perspective, he honestly thought he would recover better at home with his family and some tender loving care. I, however, was thinking about what that meant for me.

Surely, he can't come home like this. And by "this" I mean, completely paralyzed from the chest down. Honestly, my initial thoughts were fearful. Who was going to take care of him? I wasn't. I'm not equipped, trained, or remotely qualified to handle him under these circumstances. Why would he leave Magee? They had a great staff, top notch facilities, expensive accessible equipment and 24-hour bedside care.

I knew he would need a massive amount of specialized attention. He couldn't walk. He couldn't stand. He had no control of his bowels. He needed injections. He couldn't dress himself. He could barely feed himself. He was confined to a wheelchair. He needed a nurse, equipment, and a lot of medication. The list was running like a telegraph in my head. Did he take into consideration what this would mean for me? He kept saying, "You can do this Sweetah, I trust you!" The problem was that I didn't trust me. The house wasn't even ready for this level of disability, and neither was I. What was he thinking? What if he died under my care? My children and his family would blame me for the rest of their lives. That was too much pressure and I loved him too much to risk it.

I traded in my helpmate uniform, for a nurse mate and yes, there's a difference. I would have to step out of my comfort zone and operate in a higher level of love to pull this off. The voice of truth tells me to not be afraid. The truth is that my concerns are legitimate, but I decided to care for him as long as I have breath. *God did not give me a spirit of fear.* (**2 Timothy 1:7**) So I needed to shut out the voices of intimidation, of worry, of bitterness, of lack and discouragement because the power of love conquers all.

It's so hard to be a saint

Romans 12:10-1 tells us to *be kind, devoted, and authentic towards each other.*

We are to rejoice, be patient, and keep praying for strength and guidance. We are also supposed to be hospitable and contributing to the needs of others. The hardest of my responsibilities was fixing my mind. When I was not intentional about assessing my thoughts, I was overwhelmed. When I was overwhelmed, I was no good to my family, who was expecting me to keep it all together.

The burden and mental distress was easy to hide behind a smile and positive remarks. It manifested in other ways like weight gain, sleep problems, physical ailments. I felt a lot of pressure to keep things normal for the boys. Pressure to perform my duties. Pressure to keep up with the household paperwork. Pressure to not let anyone down and to stay on top of everything. Pressure to be a perfect wife and mom. Pressure to keep everyone updated on his condition and progress. I'm tired remembering all the pressure, but I handled it the best I could and through it all, I never felt any financial pressure. The more I surrendered to God, the more He worked things out.

I tried not to complain, but it was hard to be in a considerate and caring mode all day long as a caregiver. The more I was available for my husband, the less I was available for others, including myself. I constantly had to encourage him, or the dark days turned into even darker nights. I tried to be thoughtful, supportive, uplifting, and humorous, because laughter is great medicine. I tried to have an empathetic ear and bring hope to the situation, but it was hard because distressing circumstances were repeatedly inconvenient.

Sometimes when he said "thank you", I couldn't even respond due to frustration. I kept reminding myself to remain tenderhearted, because he didn't have control over the situation either. I didn't want him to feel that I was unsympathetic to his plight or be unkind with my words or deeds. It is hard to not want to cry some days. I couldn't stand to seem him struggle to do extremely basic tasks and I was so exhausted. I didn't feel pity, but I did feel a sense of sadness for what losing his legs has cost him, for what it cost my boys and our family. Imagining the inability to just jump up and walk, confined to a wheelchair year after year. It was heartbreaking and could easily lead to depression, anxiety, and other issues.

Staying Alive

Before my husband was released, after his third surgery, we took quite a few classes at the hospital in preparation for home care. He also underwent some occupational therapy that would help him with transitioning to a non-medical environment. We made some ADA (American Disabilities Act) improvements and modifications to our home instead of moving. Thank God for good health insurance benefits that covered the daily in-home care of a nurse and physical therapist. We ordered plenty of equipment to assist us in the daily routines. Supplies and prescriptions were put on a weekly and monthly ordering system.

Bayada Home Health Care provided additional training and support. My lifestyle changed drastically. I rarely left the house because he could not be left alone. So, I devised a shopping system that involved pre-purchasing small denomination gift cards to fast food restaurants and drug and local grocery stores. When kind-hearted neighbors asked what they could grab us when they were out and about, I would provide them with my list and reimburse them with a gift card. I was so grateful for their support. **I John 3:18** says that *love is not just a word, but it is also a verb.*

I had to make some hard decisions. I was used to serving full-time in ministry and within our community. It became too much to manage with our new scenario, so I resigned from all my positions. I had to limit our children's activities to no more than one sport each, per season. This required carpooling and special arrangements for them to attend practice and games. Over time, my fears subsided but I had some trusted help from a few trusted neighbors who were nurses. In the early weeks of home care, I called them to assist me when I gave him injections; hooked up IV bags; tried various catheters. After a while, I needed less assistance and became comfortable with all the new routines. I was fully committed to giving him the best care I could and keeping him alive. The goal was to eventually get him to the place of self-sufficiency, in hopes that he might return to work one day.

Some days were very l-o-n-g-g-g-g and full of expectations. I would say I cannot live like this much longer. Despite my extreme exhaustion, I pressed on and tried to do so without complaining. I made appointments. I changed the soiled sheets. I changed his diapers. I sanitized everything. I cooked and cleaned. I kept up with the kids. I administered medications. I helped with therapy. I cleaned and bathed him. I did lots of laundry. I would do his grooming. I picked up prescriptions. I fed him every meal. I was 100% available. The next day and everyday was a replay. One day I said out loud to myself, "I feel like his mother, not his wife." This is like taking care of another baby, but with man-size weight attached. He was wearing me down. Naturally, some days were more bearable than others. I would often remind myself that my sacrifice was critical in him staying alive, staying well, and staying out of the hospital, which was certainly better than being six feet under. Thank You, Lord, for your grace, your mercy, and for keeping us!

I am changing

Recently, I bumped into some old acquaintances, and most of them didn't think I changed one bit. If they looked hard enough, they would see the new me. I'm most certainly not the same woman I was a year ago, three years ago, or even seven years ago. I've changed because my circumstances have changed. Time and interaction will later reveal just how I have grown through this season.

"Like clothing, you will change them, and they shall be changed" (**Psalm 102:26 NKJV**).

I'm so thankful that the Lord loved me enough to not

leave me like I was. Change is good. Embrace it. Don't fight it. I've been through some difficult situations these last seven years as a caregiver. I've learned and grown from every single experience, while seizing every opportunity to how my husband how much I love him along the way. So, whether the day was good, bad, messy, not so messy, up, down, fresh or funky, I am thankful for every day. Although I've cried through some of those days, I realized that what doesn't break me, will only make me stronger. I am molded by my circumstances and being shaped into a new creation. So, it's all good in the end.

"If Anyone is in Christ, he is a new creation; old things have passed away; all things have become new" (2 **Corinthians 5:17, NKJV**).

Change can hurt. It can hurt your pride, your wallet, your patience, but everyone on the Potter's wheel becomes a masterpiece.

Remember ... you can do EVERYTHING through Christ who gives you strength

ABOUT THE VISIONARY

Valerie Stancill is the founder of Purposed For Wellness a holistic wellness center committed to helping people to become empowered, feel better, and live longer with a variety of holistic alternatives. Her passion is to educate, mentor, and equip people to regain control and live abundantly by changing their lifestyles.

Valerie speaks from the heart; as a caregiver to her husband for 14 years. She gave her life unconditionally for her husband and would do it again. She can empathize with these women as she has walked in their shoes. Her passion is to help women realize they can live again no matter what life throws your way. Her journey was for purpose and she will continue to walk in it until she no longer has breath in her body. Her bucket list dream is to save the world! She continues to stand in her husband's absence on their favorite scripture Jeremiah 29:11.

Valerie is an entrepreneur, health & wellness and

domestic violence advocate, radio show host on Purpose to Wellness, author, healing trauma wounds facilitator, speaker and a contributing writer for Stay Focused magazine. Valerie is also the founder of Authentic You Movement which empowers, equips, and inspires women. She believes we are here as Sista's to help another Sista...

Valerie has interviewed on gospel radio, Mixed Race Radio with Tiffany Rae Reid, CUTV News Talk Radio with Doug Llewelyn. In addition, she hosted The Master's Plan Wellness Wednesday on WTMR 800 AM. Valerie's educational background includes a BS in Health Arts from the University of St. Francis. She became certified as a holistic wellness coach through the Institute of Integrative Nutrition, licensed massage therapist through Rizzieri School of Massage, Reiki practitioner through A Loved Thing Healing Arts and a certified Yoni Steam practitioner through Total Serenity. Valerie worked in several hospitals in Philadelphia in Interventional Radiology and CAT scan departments in both management and staff positions. Valerie is also passionate in bringing awareness to Pulmonary Arterial Hypertension, the disease which caused her husband's demise. Valerie is the mother of an amazing daughter, and son-in- love and grandmother of four awesome grandsons. Valerie is available for speaking engagements, workshops, and conferences. For more information contact her at authorvstancill@gmail.com

ABOUT THE CO-AUTHORS

Charlene Yuvette Atchison was born in Buffalo New York, but now resides in Erie Pennsylvania. She attended Bennett High School and Buffalo State College to pursue an Associate Degree in Child Psychology. She is the author of Chronicles of Being Adopted , which was listed as Best Seller in her category, she has written three more books which are, Releasing The Pain, My Inner Thoughts and Shattered But Still Standing. She is also a contributing author of several anthologies and she has also a contributing author of anthology, *Women Overcome Through Writing (WOW)* and *When Healing Hurts: Living Through the Loss of a Loved One.* She has also contributed to two poetry books.

April Green is a wife, mother of three children living with Autism Spectrum Disorder (ASD) and licensed minister. April has worked in the field of early childhood special education for the past 20 years and is currently pursuing her doctorate degree in educational leadership. April has a background in psychology and Curriculum Instruction and Assessment and has a passion for early intervention and promoting awareness. This passion led April to host and produce the podcast, "Keeping it Moving with April and Vondell." which sheds light on mental health and autism awareness. April's passion to share her story and bring awareness has also led to her writing a blog called Ausome-Sauce, which chronicles experiences raising multiple children living with Autism April strongly believes that awareness is key to acceptance and is a vehicle for change, while helping others find peace and purpose through the pain.

Lorraine Goffney has been working in the law enforcement Industry for over 26 years. While she is very affluent in keeping the peace and enforcing laws and regulations, her passion is to help hurting people. God has birthed a nonprofit organization through her, True Endeavors/Our Seeds of Faith, where she is the Founder and CEO. At True Endeavors / Our Seeds of Faith, she stands side by side with her mother as they reach out to families that have lost a loved one through tragic death, mainly gun violence. Their purpose is to touch hurting families with the love of God to help them get through the grieving process and see the positive things that remain in their lives. Lorraine currently resides in New Jersey, however, being a military brat, she doesn't consider that to be her home. Her chapter in this anthology is very personal, as she is extremely connected to her story because the pain and struggle of sacrifice was the fuel that ignited her desire to live beyond her own strength. God protected her when she lost my way.

Jennifer N. Laws is a native of Philadelphia. She is a published writer, hostess, actress, producer and CEO of Top Line Divas LLC. Jennifer began her writing career in 2008 as a poet simply because she wanted to express herself. She has performed on many stages in New York, Pa., NJ and Baltimore. Tapping into her creativity she began to write personalized poems for all occasions. In addition to the stage Jennifer's work was featured on radio, and various local T.V. shows in the Tri-State Area. In 2013 her article on Domestic Violence was featured in Queen Size Magazine a topic that is near and dear to her heart. You can also find her early work on file at the Library of Congress. Recently she began to write for more media outlets like Size Overrated Magazine. Jennifer also enjoys producing as well as hosting live events and was honored to be the hostess at The Ms Delaware Pageant, The World Is My Runway Fashion Show in NY and The Living Artist Showcase in Philadelphia. Jennifer hopes to expand as a Public Speaker, Producer,Hostess and Writer.

Donna Healey is 65 years old and was born and raised in southern NJ. She grew up in a small family in a small town. After graduating HS and attending some college, she trained as an ultrasound technologist; a job that has served her well for over 42 years. She has been married for 34 years and has 30-year-old twins.

Nicole D. Muraoka is an educator, speaker, evangelist, and psalmist. She is also the Co-Founder and COO of Igniting the Flame, LLC, with headquarters in Philadelphia, Pennslyvania Nicole holds a Bachleors in Science in Business Administration with a minor in Marketing Management and currently pursuing a graduate degree in Educational Leadership. Nicole is a team player with over 15 years of management experience and over 10 years of mentoring and coaching adults. She is an encouragement and inspiration to all who know her.

Terri Robinson grew up in Washington, DC and is a graduate of Talladega College. She has worked in the public sector in various areas of human capital management - college recruitment, employee and management counseling, program and project management, and policy development, before retiring unexpectedly. Later, she combined her gifts of compassion and empathy with her various career skills to provide caregiving support to family and serves as a resource providing information and advice in caregiving management. Also, for several years Terri was an entrepreneur providing services in branding development, marketing strategies, and billing and collections. Until her mother's transition, Terri served as the primary caregiving coordinator for her. She is active in her spiritual community with youth, dance, women's fellowship, and bereavement ministries. She may be contacted at: 2TerriRobinson@gmail.com.

Tonya Brown Rivers is an inspirational author of two fiction and three nonfiction works. She resides in her hometown of Charlotte, North Carolina with her husband and two sons. She enjoys the passion of writing and sharing to not only entertain, but to sustain and reach readers. It is her hope that the words by God who is her initial editor, equips her to the opportunity to reach the masses in the platform to motivate the soul.

Vivian J. Stokes-Smallwood, a sincere woman of God, brings a special light to all those blessed to know her. Her love for God, family, and people, sums up the first and second greatest command (Matthew 22:37-39). She earned a Bachelor of Arts in Christian studies at Grand Canyon University in November 2018. She is pursuing a Master of Arts in Pastoral Counseling with a community chaplaincy focus at Liberty University. Her life endeavors garner a "ministry of presence" as a way of being available to people and listening for the call that focuses on care giving.

Maurita Lyda is a minister, transformational coach, and writer, who overcame sexual abuse. She realized that through writing and a relationship with God, she could free her pain and overcome all things. She is committed to helping women and children overcome abusive situations. Maurita is the mother of 14 children, the adoptive mother of 14 children, and has 23 grandchildren. She was born in Detroit, Michigan. Her new journal, Journey of Greatness was just released.

Tonya Holly grew up in Washington, DC, is a retail expert, writer, and University of Maryland graduate (where she met her husband). They reside in Southern New Jersey and she is passionate about training up their four amazing sons. She became a caregiver after her husband survived several spinal surgeries, which left him paralyzed. But praise God, he is not done with him yet! They minister to families through a Family Life Group at Rock Life Church and are candidates for ordination. Her monthly blog "Be-Attitudes" are simple positive attitudes you should mirror to become blessed in every area of your life. For speaking engagements, contact her at p31blessed@comcast.net and visit her website https://tonyaholly.wixsite.com/tonyaholly.

Made in the USA
Middletown, DE
28 August 2020

15415469R00083